Praise for *Full Time*

'I can only describe it as the best sports book I've read and among the most courageous ever written'
Tom Humphries, *Irish Times*

'. . . but why did Tony Cascarino want to share all this with us? We know now, and it was a privilege to have been introduced. Far more than the goals, this is Tony Cascarino's legacy to the game'
David Walsh, *Sunday Times*

'A remarkable tale . . . makes the most fascinating reading'
Daily Mail

'There has been an unusually good batch of football autobiographies this season . . . this, coming from the most unlikely source of all, is by far the best. Fantastic'
Independent

'If you only buy one football book this year make sure that it is the truly extraordinary *Full Time: The Secret Life of Tony Cascarino*'
Richard Whitehead, *The Times*

'It's a lot more intersting than David Beckham's'
Guardian

'The finest new sporting title – the most fun, the most perceptive and maybe even the best written. It's difficult to tell whether the magic of *Full Time* is the result of Cascarino's honesty or Paul Kimmage's clever prose, or both, but it has that elusive quality that publishers long for: a charm that will appeal even to those who are not passionate about the game'
Independent on Sunday

Also by Paul Kimmage

Rough Ride

To Michael and Teddy and Maeva. See you soon.
And for Mark O'Neill, fighting the bravest fight

full time

the secret life of
TONY
CASCARINO

as told to
PAUL KIMMAGE

Scribner

First published in Great Britain and Ireland by
Simon & Schuster/TownHouse, 2000
This edition published in Great Britain and Ireland by
Scribner, 2005
An imprint of Simon & Schuster UK Ltd

Simon & Schuster UK is A CBS COMPANY

Scribner and design are trademarks of Macmillan Library Reference USA, Inc.,
used under license by Simon & Schuster, the publisher of this work.

5 7 9 10 8 6

Simon & Schuster UK Ltd
1st Floor
222 Gray's Inn Road
London WC1X 8HB

www.simonandschuster.co.uk

Simon & Schuster Australia
Sydney

A CIP catalogue record for this book is available from the British Library

ISBN-13: 978-0-7432-8531-5

Printed and bound by
CPI Group (UK) Ltd, Croydon, CR0 4YY

Contents

Chapter One
Nancy in the Morning

When you're young, you always feel that life hasn't yet begun – that 'life' is always scheduled to begin next week, next month, next year, after the holidays – whenever. But then suddenly you're old and the scheduled life didn't arrive. You find yourself asking 'Well then, exactly what was it I was having – that interlude – the scrambly madness – all that time I had before?'

– Douglas Coupland, *Life After God*

I open my eyes to the sound of my hometown, Nancy, in the morning: the 7.43 a.m. for Paris pulling out slowly from the station; the hum of exhaust pipes on the avenue de la Garenne; an ambulance klaxoning moronically in the distance; heavy drops of rain rapping the bedroom window and beyond the white net curtain, the first sight of Nancy, an eternal grey sky, always the same.

Virginia is sleeping. I reach out and nudge her gently and watch her blink and stretch and slowly stir to life. No words are exchanged between us as she pulls on her dressing gown and trudges towards the door. I lie with my thoughts and listen to the sound of Maeva being woken and coaxed into the bathroom: *'Allez, Maeva, c'est l'heure, ma cherie.'* I pull back the sheets and swivel my legs on to the floor. My knee, as usual, has seized during the night. I run my fingers across the joint and feel the bone and cartilage grinding like a rusty old gate. The first step of the day is always the most painful. First, I lift

1

my heel off the floor and flex my leg gently. Then, placing my hands on the side of the bed for the launch, I push forward, taking the weight on my left leg and hold the post of the bed for support. By the time I have limped from the wardrobe to the bathroom to the kitchen, I am almost walking normally. Virginia hands me a cup of tea. Maeva has breakfasted and is ready for school.

My name is Tony Cascarino and I am thirty-seven years old. I live with Maeva Cascarino and Virginia Masson on the third floor of an apartment block, a short walk from Nancy train station at 6 avenue de la Garenne. Madame Ginet, a mild-mannered teacher who sometimes teaches me French, lives in the apartment above. Monsieur Madaous, a bad-tempered sales rep who almost always acts like a prick (whenever Maeva is loud or I absentmindedly obstruct his parking space), lives in the apartment below. It is not, by any means, an exclusive development. We buy our groceries from the Codec store around the corner, drop our rubbish on the ground floor in a bin behind the lift and collect our post from wooden boxes bearing our names in the entrance hall. Most of the tenants are office workers, secretaries or tradesmen – ordinary people living ordinary lives . . . well, maybe mine is a little different.

I play football with Nancy Football Club or L'Association Sportif Nancy-Lorraine (ASNL), as it is more properly known. I have been a professional footballer since 1982, when I walked off a building site in London one afternoon and signed for a third-division team called Gillingham. Before working on the building site, I spent two years cutting and styling women's hair. Professional football is a lot more fun than building or hairdressing. It also pays better and carries a lot more perks: we travel first-class, stay in the best hotels, eat the finest food, wear designer clothes, drive the fastest cars and never have to queue for surgeons, doctors or dentists. The game is good to us. The game is everything you dream it is: we are worshipped like pop stars, pampered and spoiled. But after nineteen years, it begins to wear you down. Of late the sheer boredom of playing and training has been killing me. Sometimes, on the night before a game, I lie on the five-star bed in the five-star hotel and gaze at the five-star ceiling and it feels like a prison cell. But I still get anxious when the manager names the team. I still get excited when Saturday comes.

My daughter, Maeva, is five years old. When she throws her arms around me and calls me 'Papa', it is easily the nicest thing anyone has ever said to me. She was born in Nice in August 1995 at a time when I was married to another woman, living in another place and leading a deceitful double life. A day old when I sneaked away and saw her for the first time, she was aware of me for the first year of her life as the father who slept with her mother but never stayed the night.

The L'École Maternelle de Notre-Dame is a ten-minute drive from the apartment. We take the lift to the ground floor and skip quickly through the rain to the car, where our warm breath soon mists the windscreen.

'*On peut rien voir,*' Maeva protests, as we join the queue on avenue de la Garenne.

'I know, Mimi,' I reply. 'I've switched on the fan to clear it.'

'*Ça marche pas, papa.*'

'It will clear in a moment, Mimi. Sit back and put on your seat belt.'

'*D'accord.*'

D'accord is French for OK. Maeva knows *d'accord* is French for OK and knows the English for pretty much everything she says but refuses to converse with me in anything but French. Still, we understand each other perfectly and communicate just fine except on the subject of the school canteen. Maeva doesn't like the school canteen; spoiled rotten by her adoring (but somewhat bourgeois) great-grandmother, she can't understand why they never serve smoked salmon or change the plates after each course and insists we take her home for lunch. This morning's argument was pretty typical . . .

'Don't forget to tell your teacher you're eating in the canteen today.'

'*J'aime pas la cantine.*'

'Yes, I know, but you have to eat there today.'

'*Hier j'ai vomi.*'

'Yes, I know, but you'll be all right today. You can eat and have a sleep in the afternoon and later I will come and collect you. Is that a deal?'

She crosses her arms and refuses to answer. We crawl past the train station and into rue Mazegran.

'*Papa, j'ai oublié de me laver mes dents.*'

'That's not very good, is it? You'll have teeth like bombed houses. Do you want some music on?'

'*Oui.*'

'What would you like?'

'Ehhh . . . Joe Dassin.'

'Joe Dassin! What, no English music! How about some Lisa Stansfield? How about a good old Rochdale girl?'

'*J'aime pas English.*'

'OK, we'll play some froggy stuff, then. Which Joe Dassin song would you like? "*Salut les Amoureux*", "*Le Petit Pain au Chocolat*" or "*L'été Indien*"?'

' "*Salut les Amoureux*".'

'Yeah, I like that.'

'*Plus fort, papa. J'entends rien!*'

'OK, calm down.'

I find a vacant space near the school on rue de la Ravinelle and lead Maeva by the hand to the entrance. Other parents are dropping children off; from the look in their eye as we exchange '*bonjours*', it is clear to me that they know who I am. The recognition is flattering. Although I have never felt that comfortable in the spotlight, one of the real satisfactions of my life these days is when Maeva comes home from school glowing because her dad has been mentioned in class. They call me 'Tony Goal' in these parts, which will probably sound absurd if you happen to follow football and live in Birming-ham, Glasgow or London. But it's true. Only six other players can boast a better strike rate this season in the French first division. My name will ring a bell in every village Café des Sports. But it is also true that when it comes to much of what happened before, I can offer little by way of defence.

Ten years ago, in what seems another life, I moved from Millwall to Aston Villa, at a time when Villa were top of the league and closing on the championship. Brilliant since the start of the season, the team had started to falter in March and I was bought to supply the goals that would stave off Liverpool. I didn't score for seven games. Liverpool were champions. Villa finished runners-up. A year later, I moved from Villa to Glasgow Celtic but the drought continued. One afternoon, I was out shopping with my pregnant wife and my son Michael when a supporter stopped me in the street and offered a critical assessment.

'You're fucking shit, you,' he hissed. 'You're a useless big bastard.' Glasgow is the world capital of tribal hatred and friends had warned me not to react when approached by Rangers fans, but this fellow was absolutely raving. 'You're a fucking wanker, a useless bastard.'

'Look, mate,' I pleaded, 'give me a break. Can't you see I'm with my wife and son?'

'You're fucking shit,' he said. 'And I'm a Celtic fan.'

We moved to London six months later but the cataclysm continued at Chelsea. I was booed at Stamford Bridge on the day I made my début, and then Michael came home from school one afternoon and inflicted the cruellest blow of all. The boys in his class had been talking about me. 'You're not very good, Dad, are you?' he said. How do you respond to something like that? What do you say to your six-year-old son? That his friends are wrong? That there's a lot more to the game than what they hear from their dads? What's your defence when you're thirty-one years old and your career is in freefall? There was nothing to do but swallow hard and resolve to make him proud.

FULL TIME

Six years have passed since I left England's shores and whenever I return, people who remember me as the lanky striker who used to play for Gillingham often stop me in the street and ask what I'm doing now. Unfortunately, the French sports daily *L'Equipe* doesn't sell that well in Chislehurst; I might as well be scoring goals on Mars. Usually, I'll fob them off with some yarn about retirement. How do I begin to explain my secret life? There is so much they would never understand.

I remind Maeva again about the canteen and brave the rain back to the car. Joe Dassin has moved on to '*L'Été Indien*'. Indian summer! Not in this part of France. It is October and Nancy is cold and sad and grey, and over the next five months it won't change much. Take away the magnificence of the place Stanislas and Nancy doesn't have a lot going for it. The people are decent but struggle to make a living. If it were England, it would be Barnsley.

Heading west from the city towards the suburb of Laxou, I take the A31 towards the training ground at Forêt de Haye. The manager has announced a double session today. Double sessions are murder when it's cold and wet and you've got bombed cartilage for a knee. I've had two cortisone injections already this season. For the last eight years I've taken anti-inflammatory pills before and after every game. The pills play havoc with my stomach and scorch my arse with diarrhoea but when the ball hits the back of the net and the crowd chants my name, it seems a small price to pay. How much longer can I keep paying? I don't know. There isn't a week that goes by these days when I don't ask myself that question, knowing the answer will always be the same. I play football because I have to play football. I play football because I know nothing else. On the first Friday of every month, the incentive to keep going is dropped through my letterbox in printed type: allowances and bonuses, taxes and fines, all listed in francs and centimes.

I earn FF160,000 a month playing for Nancy, which, depending on bonuses, translates to roughly £8,000 a month after tax. Pretty much everything we spend is budgeted for these days – a sharp contrast to my youth, when the only figures that mattered were the goal-scoring stats. But you change as you get older: you worry about the future more. Last week, after another night spent tossing and turning, I sat down with a pen and paper and tried to figure it all out.

1982	Gillingham	£9,200
1983	Gillingham	10,400
1984	Gillingham	13,000
1985	Gillingham	£13,000
1986	Gillingham	£13,000
1987	Gillingham/Millwall	£20,800
1988	Millwall	£23,400
1989	Millwall	£26,000
1990	Millwall/Aston Villa	£56,000
1991	Aston Villa/Celtic	£71,500
1992	Celtic/Chelsea	£78,000
1993	Chelsea	£78,000
1994	Chelsea/Marseilles	£147,000
1995	Marseilles	£225,000
1996	Marseilles	£199,000
1997	Nancy	£126,000
1998	Nancy	£98,400
1999	Nancy	£140,000
Approximate income from football since 1982		£1,347,700
Bonus payments and sign-on fees since 1982		£967,000
Total career earnings since 1982		£2,314,700

It was a sobering experience. Two point three million! Where the hell has it all gone! I mean, there are porters and plumbers and painters who win that on the lottery and never have to work again. They buy a dream house and a dream car and take their holiday of a lifetime and never look back. They probably won't, it's fair to say, invest as heavily in their pension . . .

$$
\begin{array}{r}
£2,314,700 \\
-£150,000 \\
\hline
£2,164,700
\end{array}
$$

. . . and definitely won't, it's true to say, give 40 per cent away in tax . . .

$$
\begin{array}{r}
£2,164,700 \\
-£870,040 \\
\hline
£1,294,660
\end{array}
$$

. . . or get slapped with agents' fees . . .

$$
\begin{array}{r}
£1,294,660 \\
-£32,000 \\
\hline
£1,262,660
\end{array}
$$

They won't sign for Celtic and drop thirty-five grand in Birmingham because they bought just before the property crash . . .

$$
\begin{array}{r}
£1,262,660 \\
-£35,000 \\
\hline
£1,227,660
\end{array}
$$

. . . but they may incur the unfortunate sting of divorce . . .

$$
\begin{array}{r}
£1,227,660 \\
-£200,000 \\
\hline
£1,027,660
\end{array}
$$

. . . with its maintenance payments that click like a taxi meter . . .

$$
\begin{array}{r}
£1,027,660 \\
-£24,000 \\
\hline
£1,003,660
\end{array}
$$

NANCY IN THE MORNING

. . . and school fees . . .

$$£1,003,660$$
$$-£18,000$$
$$£985,660$$

. . . not to mention the tip for the solicitors . . .

$$£985,660$$
$$-£5,000$$
$$£980,660$$

And when you add it all up, or rather take it all away, nine hundred grand is not a lot of jam when spread over what it costs to live for eighteen years. And it certainly hasn't insured my happy-ever-afters. So you keep fighting the pain when you step out of bed each morning. And you keep taking the pills that rot your stomach and burn your arse. And you keep putting the dye in your hair and pretending you're ten years younger. You survive. You do what you can. But on mornings like this when the rain is lashing the windscreen, it's hard.

That Celtic fan who insulted me in Glasgow, the supporters at Stamford Bridge who derided me for fun – I wish they could have been there on the night I beat Juventus. I wish they could have heard the cheers of the most fanatical supporters in France. I wish they could have seen what I went on to. I swallowed hard. I turned it around. I tried to make Michael proud. Did I? Yes, I'd like to think I did.

His mother, Sarah, is writing a novel at the moment. It's the story of a young woman who loves and loses and is forced to start again. The woman, who is also called Sarah, lives in a leafy suburb of London with her husband Eric and their two young sons. Eric is a professional footballer whose career is falling apart. Unwanted and unloved, he is on the verge of quitting the game when he is thrown a lifeline by a big club in

France. They find a house in Aix-en-Provence and at first struggle to adapt but within months are embracing the joy of their new lives. For Eric, it's the discovery of what he knew he always had. For Sarah, it's the smell and feel of Provence and their new way of life. The boys settle, too, and seem happy at school. Sarah has never been as content. It's a new chapter. The chance to start again. And then, incredibly, it all falls apart . . .

It happens unexpectedly, on the evening of an international game in Dublin. Sarah has returned to London to spend a few days with her mum, when a friend, whose husband, like hers, also plays for the Republic of Ireland, suggests they take a late flight to Dublin to 'surprise the boys'. The game has ended when their flight from Gatwick touches down. They take a taxi to the team hotel and arrive to find their husbands celebrating with the manager and rest of the team in the bar. Eric seems pleased. He calls a porter and has her bags delivered to his room and suggests they go for a meal. They retire with their friends to the dining room. Sarah places her order and asks Eric for the key to the room. She enters the room and sits down to call her mum. There is nothing to worry about. Her precious boys are safely tucked in bed. She thanks her mum and swivels away from the desk, tipping over a small bin with her foot. A crumpled sheet of fax paper tumbles on to the carpet. She picks it up and is about to toss it back when curiosity tempts her to unravel it. The fax is from a woman. The woman is French. The woman is pregnant. The woman has just had a scan and is expecting a baby girl. Eric is about to become a father again.

Shaking with rage, she storms back to the dining room and an embarrassing scene ensues. Eric pleads for calm and ushers his wife back to the room. Dismissing the affair as a brief encounter, he begs her forgiveness and promises never to see the other woman again. They return to France and after a few difficult weeks the relationship settles down and appears to return to normal. But behind Sarah's back, Eric continues to lie and cheat. One morning, after dropping the boys at school, she returns to find a note on the kitchen table. 'I'm sorry, Sarah. I know you will never understand but it was something I had to do. Eric.' She checks the bedroom: her husband has removed his clothes. She collapses on the bed in a flood of tears, shaking with grief and anger. The bastard! The cruel, spineless, swine! What is to become of them? Where will they live? How will she explain it to the boys? What breed of man uproots his family from everything they know and abandons them in a strange land?

I'm not sure how the story ends or what Sarah intends to call the book when it's published. I'd like to think that, it being a work of fiction, any resemblance between its characters and real people is purely coincidental. I'd like to think that Michael will read it and never confuse Eric with his dad. I'd like to think he goes to school these days with the cuttings he gets from his nan and says 'Told you so' to his mates. I'd like to think he sleeps beneath my poster on his bedroom wall. I'd like to think he understands. But what I'd like to think and what I do think, are not the same.

There's a gendarme parked in the usual spot on the slip-road off the motorway. I scramble for my safety belt and sling it hastily across my waist; he smiles and waves me through. I take the first exit off the roundabout and the first left into Parc de Haye, where the training ground car park is almost deserted except for the manager's Mercedes and one or two of the ground staff. I am early this morning, but then I am almost always early. At my age, it pays to convey enthusiasm, even when you don't always feel it. No, at my age it is *essential* to convey enthusiasm, *especially* when you don't always feel it. Just another little trick in the art of staying employed.

Eighteen years in football. How swiftly the seasons pass. When I was just starting out at Gillingham, there was a player called Dick Tydeman who had spent most of his career at Charlton and was the same age, or pretty close, as I am now.

Dick was in fantastic condition and still leading most of the runs and I remember sidling up to him at training one morning and marvelling at his enthusiasm. He looked at me and smiled and snapped his fingers: 'Make the most of it,' he said, 'because it's going to go like that. One morning you'll wake up and think, "That was my football career."' How right he was. Sometimes, when I look back at old photographs I hardly recognize myself. Whatever happened to Dick Tydeman? I wonder what he's doing now?

Nothing keeps me awake more at night than the fear of what happens next. A recent conversation I had with Jack Charlton is a source of recurring bad dreams.

'Ah, Cassy, don't tell me you're still turning up,' he smiled, when we met in the lobby of a Dublin hotel on the eve of an international. 'What are you going to do after football?'

'I don't know yet, Jack,' I replied.

'What do you mean, you don't know! You've been doing the same thing for eighteen years – you must have some ideas.'

'No, Jack, I'm not sure.'

'What about taking your coaching badge?'

'Well . . . yeah . . . but I'm not sure I want to go down the football road, Jack.'

'You've got to do something. It's the only thing you know.'

'Yeah, but not everyone wants to do what you did, Jack.'

'Why not? Tell me what, then?'

'Well, at the moment I've invested some money in a house in Tahiti and I'm trying to get that off the ground.'

'A house! Tahiti! That's not going to keep you going for more than a few months, is it? What are you going to do in the long term?'

'I don't know, Jack. Everything you're saying makes perfect sense but at the moment I just don't know.'

My current contract with Nancy expires in June when, overnight, my status will change from eight-grand-a-month-superstar to unemployed. Should I keep scoring goals between now and the end of the season, there's a fair chance the club will offer me an extension. And that will be the real dilemma: I don't want another contract and I've had my fill of the game, but when it comes to the crunch, I'm not sure I'll have the courage to turn the offer down. A former team mate called the other day and asked if I knew of anyone who could get him tickets for the European Championships. He earns his living these days as a corporate ticket tout. Others I have played with, former internationals, are driving delivery vans and selling cars. Year after year, you convince yourself there'll be something around the corner, some opportunity you hadn't considered, some unexpected offer from Sky television, until finally you reach the end and there's nothing there.

I step from the car and cross the gravel to the changing room, where my kit has been laid out neatly on the bench. The room is empty and hollow and peaceful. I sit for a moment and close my eyes in the silence, then reach for my boots and drop them on the floor. Nancy in the morning; eternal grey.

Chapter Two
Little Voice

Doubt, it seems to me, is the central condition of a human being in the twentieth century.

– Salman Rushdie

The drive to Luxemburg takes seventy-five minutes. I find a space in the long-term car park, button my coat against the cold and make the short walk to the Luxair desk in the departures hall. A couple of businessmen travelling to Manchester for the day are standing in a queue. After checking in, I proceed directly to the departures hall and hand my passport and boarding pass to the stern-looking officer at the control. He flicks the passport open, glances at my face and checks it against the photograph inside. Although I have terrorized the odd defence in my time and was once captured by a Scottish photographer in the car park at Celtic with a balaclava on, I have never been a member of an illegal organization, but I am often subjected to scrutiny at border control. It's the details they find confusing. I can tell sometimes when they check my passport that they can't join the dots . . .

Passport: IRELAND
Surname: Cascarino
Forename(s): Anthony Guy
Date of birth: 01/Sep 1962
Date of issue: 08/Oct 1996
Nationality: Irish
Place of birth: GBR

LITTLE VOICE

Can an English-born Italian with an Irish passport travelling to Ireland via England really be that confusing? Well, maybe just a bit.

It is Thursday, 11 November. After a short stop in Manchester, it is just after midday when the flight lands in Dublin. Not much confusion as to my identity here; people nod and wave as I make my way to the baggage hall. I collect my bag from the belt, sling it across my shoulder and exit via the blue channel at customs control. Anything to declare? Not much . . .

1 set of car keys
1 passport
1 wallet
1 mobile phone + charger
1 toilet bag
4 team-issue Umbro T-shirts.
2 pairs of Addidas football (moulded and studs) boots
1 pair of shin pads
1 team-issue Umbro track suit
4 pairs of socks
4 pairs of pants
1 magazine (*FHM*) purchased at Manchester airport.
1 book (*The Guv'nor* by Lenny McLean)

The Posthouse Hotel is a mile at most from the terminal. There was a time, not so long ago, when I'd take a taxi or call the shuttle, but lately I prefer to make the journey on foot. A sharp breeze catches my breath as I exit the terminal. I turn right past the taxi rank and walk against the traffic towards the big sweeping bend, where the friendly face of a former team mate stirs the memory as I turn for home. I glance towards the hotel and the bedroom we once shared and the spirit of Andy Townsend is chastizing me from the window: 'Oi! It's only a fiver by taxi, you tight git!' I smile and look again but he is gone.

FULL TIME

The absence of the coach from the car park tells me the team are still training. I collect my key from reception and descend to my room, which looks as if it has just been burgled. Niall Quinn's fingerprints are everywhere. The Sunderland striker has had the run of the place since Monday when, normally, I should have joined the team, but I've been struggling with my knee of late and Nancy wouldn't release me until after we'd played (and lost) last night's game to Monaco. I thread my way through the debris and decide to freshen up with a bath when Niall returns from training.

'Well, if it isn't the superstar,' he smiles. 'Don't mind the rest of us – you just turn up whenever you like.' We shake hands and chat for a while about the team and exchange gossip about Nancy and Sunderland. He tells me he has picked up a slight strain in his neck.

How can a man called Tony Cascarino play football for the Republic of Ireland? Good question. Ask the punters at Stamford Bridge and they'll say, 'Well, 'e wasn't going to play for Italy, now, was he?' A touch cruel perhaps, but undeniably true. I did qualify to play for Italy but then I qualified to play for England and Scotland as well. Why did I choose the Republic of Ireland? Well, to be honest, I suppose because they chose me. I qualified for the team in 1985 under the 'grandparents' rule. My mother, Theresa O'Malley, was the youngest of four daughters born to Agnes and Michael Joseph O'Malley, a native of Westport, County Mayo, who emigrated to London in his teens. Because we were closer to the O'Malleys than the Cascarinos, I grew up with a strong sense of 'Irishness' and got to know Michael quite well when he came to live with us for a few years after Agnes passed away. He was old and almost blind. An earpiece connected to the radio was his umbilical cord to the outside world and time. Every day, when the news was announced at 12.30 p.m., he'd look at his watch and say 'Oh, it's twelve-thirty. Sure we'll go and have a black and tan,' and I'd escort him to our local, the Bull. He died in 1982, three years

16

before I made my début for the Republic. Sometimes, I wonder what he would have made of it all . . .

Chris Byrne calls at the hotel in the afternoon and I join him in the lobby for a drink. Chris is from Dublin and works for Aer Lingus and has been a friend for years. We chat about the game and the mood among the fans and he informs me I've been getting a lot of stick from the press. I smile and pretend to shrug it off but I have always been sensitive to criticism and it stings like a festering sore for the rest of the evening. Two years have passed since my last international goal for Ireland; I was a 'wonderful servant to the team' then, 'a faithful old warrior still prepared to give his all', but the tide has been turning slowly ever since. It's the little things you notice: the kids running past you with autograph books; the look you get sometimes after a bad result; talk radio shows you just happen to tune into . . .

'We've got John from Mullingar on the line. John, you want to make a point about Tony Cascarino?'

'Yes, thanks, Des. I just thought he was a disgrace against Croatia, a complete waste of time! I can't understand why McCarthy has brought him in again.'

And the case for the defence? Well, beyond the fact that I am thirty-seven years old and still trying my best, there is none. Two years ago, I was on the verge of retiring from international football after we just failed to qualify for France '98 but I decided to keep going when Ireland's manager Mick McCarthy asked me to think about it. Still rebuilding after the Jack Charlton years, he didn't have another big centre forward to call on and needed a standby targetman for Niall Quinn. I've won twelve caps since and come off the bench for ten of them but haven't complained. Physically, I can't do it for ninety minutes any more – I play these days in fits and spurts. And maybe I was wrong to hang on and should have let go but I am one goal short of the all-time scoring record, and, like the boxer who passes his sell-by date, you always think you can do it one more time. But I won't this time. This week, we play Turkey at Lansdowne Road and again four days later in Bursa, to decide who gets to travel to the European Championships next summer. Win, lose or draw, I won't be travelling with them. John from Mullingar can sleep easily. This is my last week with the team.

I wake at eight on the morning of the game, splash some water on my face and tiptoe out of the room. Niall is sleeping; Niall is always sleeping; Niall sleeps more than anyone I've ever known. I joke sometimes that rooming with him is like rooming with a big baby. 'Right, Niall, I'll change your nappy and give you your bottle and put you down and then feed you again first thing in the morning.' It's a notion that always makes him laugh, but it's true.

The breakfast room is deserted except for Mick Byrne, the team physio; Charlie O'Leary, the team kit man; Tony Hickey, the team bodyguard; Ian Evans, the assistant team manager; and Alan McLoughlin, the only player up. It's funny, but I must have breakfasted with Alan on every morning of every trip since he joined the squad nine years ago. And yet, despite the fact that we are both early risers and ideally suited, we've never shared a room. When reminded of this, he jokes that we will have to set it right next time, knowing that there may not be a next time. If we don't beat Turkey, Alan also intends to call it a day.

After breakfast, we sit and chat and scan the morning papers. A massive earthquake measuring 7.2 on the Richter scale has rocked north-west Turkey, killing hundreds ... Andrea Curry, an Irish aid volunteer, has died in a plane crash near Kosovo ... The IRA has set a deadline to hand over some weapons ... the popstar Gary Glitter has been jailed for four months for downloading child pornography on the Internet ... the singer Shane Lynch of Boyzone is in trouble with the National Parents Association for swearing at the MTV awards ... and Mick McCarthy has named his team for the big game at

LITTLE VOICE

Lansdowne Road: Alan Kelly, Stephen Carr, Gary Breen, Kenny Cunningham, Denis Irwin, Rory Delap, Lee Carsley, Roy Keane, Kevin Kilbane, Niall Quinn and Robbie Keane. I am listed among the subs. Mark Lawrenson, whose column in the *Irish Times* I always read, thinks it a positive selection: 'If Kilbane can get forward and Delap can leave space for Carr, the visitors can be put under serious pressure out on the flanks. If that happens Niall Quinn, who is playing as well these days as I have ever seen him play, can be even more of a problem for the Turks.' All a little too highbrow for the tabloids, who, predictably, see the game as a simple case of 'stuffing the turkey'.

After two hours of lounging over breakfast, at half-past ten I return to the room where, no great surprise, Niall is still sleeping. I pull the curtains, fart and make a few loud noises: 'Look at the state of you! What are you like!' He twists and groans but dozes off again. Finally, there is nothing for it but to switch on the telly and give him a prod: 'Come on, Rip Van Winkle, you big fat bastard. Ireland is depending on you tonight!' He opens his eyes and grins and dozes until eleven, when he begins his day with a long, hot, soak in the bath.

Before lunch, we board the coach and drive to the beach at Malahide for the traditional match-day stroll. We split up into twos and threes, and I join up with Roy Keane and enquire about the latest dressing-room gossip from the most famous club in the world, Manchester United. He smiles and suggests I've come to the wrong man. 'My problem,' he says, 'is that I can never remember who I'm not talking to; I have a go at so many people during games that I can never remember next day who I'm not talking to. And who's not talking to me.' I laugh and shake my head; typical Roy.

I first got to know Roy on a trip to Boston, just after he'd made his international début in 1991. It was at a time when Jack Charlton was God in Ireland and the team was at its height. We played the USA in a friendly and drew 1–1 and then

19

hit the town, where a great night was had by all until the alarm call next morning. Some didn't go to bed. Shattered and dishevelled, we crawled on to the coach in various states of undress. A 7.30 a.m. departure was delayed until 7.45 a.m. and then 8.00 a.m., when everyone was accounted for except Roy. Jack was seething and immediately dispatched Mick Byrne to try and locate him. 'Fucking hell! Nineteen years old, his first trip away and he is nowhere to be found!' Ten minutes later, when he finally arrived, Jack went for him. 'Where the fuck have you been? Do you have any idea how long we've been waiting?' It was an absolute savaging but Roy didn't blink: 'I didn't ask you to wait, did I?' And that was it. End of confrontation. He walked straight by and sat down. We couldn't believe it. No one stood up to Jack like that! It was incredible. We were absolutely pissing ourselves. Thankfully, he has matured a great deal since, although it's still quite easy to form the wrong impression of Roy. He demands a lot on the field and can be abrasive and difficult to play with when you don't measure up to his standards, but he's a very bright fellow and has a good sense of humour when you get to know him. Not that I would ever claim to know him. The only people who really know Roy Keane are his family in Cork, but we have always got on well.

'Have you made any decision about your contract yet?' I ask. 'Are you going to sign?'

'Naah,' he says. 'I'm just taking each game as it comes for the moment. I've left all the negotiating to Michael Kennedy [his solicitor]. What about you? Are you going to play for another year?'

'I'm not sure. I don't want to, but I haven't a clue what I'll do if I stop. I'm just playing every game as if it was my last.'

We return to the hotel for lunch and retire to our rooms for the afternoon. After a few games of cards, I leave Niall to his afternoon nap and tour the other rooms in desperation for a chat but everyone is either reading or sleeping or watching telly, so I end up in the physio's room with Mick Byrne and

Charlie O'Leary. Charlie throws me a Snickers and suggests a cup of tea. Mick invites me to take a seat.

'The very man,' he says.

'Why's that, Mick?'

'Charlie, wasn't I just talking about him?'

'Just a second ago,' Charlie says.

'Cas, you're not going to believe the dream I had last night!'

'Try me.'

'I think it was a premonition!'

'About what?'

'*The game, of course*! I dreamt it was 0–0 in the eighty-eighth minute and things were looking desperate for us. Denis wins the ball just inside our half, plays a one-two with Roy and races down the wing to the byline, where he delivers this beautiful cross. The Turks have pulled everyone back to secure the vital draw but despite being heavily outnumbered, one green shirt climbs high above the sea of red and heads majestically into the net! Well, the crowd go absolutely berserk. The player races to acknowledge the roar but is engulfed by a group of stewards who have ecstatically abandoned their posts . . .' He pauses and fixes me with a grin. 'You'll never guess who the player was,' he says.

'It has to have been Niall,' I smile.

He raises my arm and gives me a hug. Charlie pours the tea.

The day runs smoothly until just before the pre-match meal, when I bump into Packie Bonner in the corridor. Packie, a friend and former team mate, is a member of the coaching staff.

'I don't think Niall is right,' he says, grimly. 'Get ready to play.'

'You're joking.'

'No, we've just had him down with Martin [the team doctor, Martin Walsh]. They're talking about a painkiller before the game.'

I continue on towards the dining room but feel the blood draining from my face. I think, 'Oh shit! I might be playing this game,' and within two seconds, the little voice is in my head . . .

'*You pathetic fucker, Cascarino!*'

'*What do you mean?*'

'*I heard what you thought.*'

'*No . . . I . . .*'

'*John from Mullingar was right, you're a fucking disgrace.*'

'*I didn't mean it like that. It just . . . .slipped out.*'

'*The truth always does.*'

'*What truth?*'

'*You don't want to play.*'

'*Of course I want to play. I was out of bed at six the other morning to drive to Luxemburg; I'll be chewing anti-inflammatories for a week for this team! Why would I inflict that on myself if I didn't want to play?*'

'*Well, I can think of the £900 match fee for a start.*'

'*That's bollocks – it has nothing to do with the money.*'

'*Oh, so you don't need the money?*'

'*I didn't say that. I said it has nothing to do with money.*'

'*So what's your problem, then?*'

'*You wouldn't understand.*'

'*No, you're right, I wouldn't. In fact, I can't think of any self-respecting professional anywhere in the world who would think what you've just thought!*'

'*I didn't mean it like that . . . Look . . . Niall Quinn has been my direct rival on this team for the last fourteen years and although he has been the preferred choice for most of that time, I never considered myself inferior to him and always believed I could do as good a job for Ireland until last year, when for the first time ever I travelled to Dublin hoping I'd be named as a sub.*'

'*Why?*'

'*I'd gone. I'd lost it. I'd started the season well with Nancy and was still training hard but the years had finally caught up with me and I didn't want to let anyone in Ireland down. Niall is four years younger than me and playing better than*

ever. I'm happy to stay involved but in a supporting role.'
    'So, it looks like you're in trouble, then?'
    'How do you mean?'
    'His neck injury sounds serious.'
    'Yeah, I can't believe it! He seemed fine this morning.'
    'Well, maybe he will be OK?'
    'I hope so.'
    'And maybe you'll get on for the last twenty minutes.'
    'Yeah, that would be great.'
    'And miss a sitter to win the game.'
    'Clear off! Give me a break.'

Think positive? Not me. I think negative. I have always been a negative person. I have always thought negative thoughts. For as long as I can remember, there has been a little voice in my head that highlights my weaknesses and undermines my confidence.

When it comes to the art of shooting oneself in the foot, I have always been world class. I think too much during the games. Most players analyse performance after a game; not me: I do it all the wrong way – I think about how I'm playing as I play. Three bad passes and I'm glancing at the touchline . . .
    'Your number's up, Tony.'
    'No it's not.'
    'One more pass like that and it will be.'

I've scored and played brilliantly one week and gone out and been awful the next, purely because some negative thought has hijacked me. I've tried to change and purge the doubt but it has always been in there, always been part of me. It was Graham Taylor at Aston Villa who noticed it first. He didn't know me from Adam when he signed me from Millwall, but within a few weeks he had identified my weakness. 'I want you to see a sports psychologist,' he said, one morning after training. 'You should be much more confident about who you are and what you want to be. I can't believe you're so negative in your approach.' A few weeks later he was offered the England job and I never followed it up. Would 'therapy' have made a difference? Perhaps, but I was quite immature at the time and wouldn't have been prepared to open up. We all know what happens in the psychiatrist's chair. Tell me about your childhood. What sort of a man was your dad? Tell me about the voice and when you first heard it. The prodding and probing of the secret corners; the paring away of the layers until your vulnerability is exposed . . .

We leave the hotel at six. A police escort speeds our passage through the streets, which are humming with the buzz of the game and Saturday night fever. I sit, gazing out of the window of the coach as we drive to the ground, struck, as always, by the silence, and reminded of the opening scene of *Saving Private Ryan* and the tension on the boats as they sped toward the beaches. As we approach Lansdowne Road, a large group of supporters have gathered outside the Shelbourne House and raise their pints in salute as we pass, unaware of our private fear and how lucky they are. Superstitious, I choose my usual spot in the corner of the dressing room and change in the usual order – shorts, shirt, socks, boots, shin pads. Charlie has hung a number twelve shirt on my peg; I change and follow Denis Irwin on to the pitch for the warm-up. Normally, when a substitute, I am relaxed before a game, but today, since my brief encounter with Packie, I've been agitated and unable to concentrate. Niall's neck has been dominating my thoughts. Painkilling injections before a game have never worked for me; you take them in the hope that the discomfort will clear with the first surge of adrenaline but it rarely does. I watch for his emergence from the dressing room and analyse his every step during our warm-up routine. It is obvious he isn't right.

'How bad is it?' I ask.

'Dunno,' he frowns.

'Just start the game and see how it goes.'

He disappears down the tunnel to get ready; I follow a few minutes later and find an anxious Mick McCarthy waiting at the door. The manager has also been observing Niall during the warm-up: 'Get yourself out there, quick,' he orders. 'You're playing. Change your shirt.' There are five minutes to kick-off. My head begins to panic . . .

'Ho ho, you're in real trouble now, old son.'

'Get lost, you twisted fuck. I haven't time.'

My heart begins to race. I rip the twelve shirt from my back and look instinctively to the peg for the nine but the peg is bare – Niall hasn't taken it off. I cross the room and find him sitting with his head between his hands, staring dejectedly at the tiles. Unsure how to ask for the shirt from his back, I fidget awkwardly for a moment in front of him until at last he senses my presence: 'Oh yeah . . . Jeeze . . . sorry, Cas.' He hands me the shirt and I slip it quickly over my head and join the rest of the team in the tunnel. We walk on to the pitch to a deafening roar from the crowd and as the national anthems are played, I drill myself to be positive and to really give it a shout. When the game begins we make a good positive start. Kevin Kilbane goes close with a couple of fine efforts and we are lifted by the reaction of the crowd. Just before half-time, Stephen Carr whips over a free kick from the right and the ball is knocked down for me by Gary Breen. For a moment, just a moment, the target opens before me like a rerun of Mick Byrne's dream. I catch the ball sweetly on the half-volley and believe I am about to score, but the goalkeeper's reaction is sensational and he deflects the shot away. And then the voice is back again. That one missed chance is enough to set him off . . .

'Hard luck, Cas. Good effort.'

'Thanks.'

'You've started really well tonight.'

'Yeah, I'm up for it.'

'So are the crowd! What an atmosphere! They would have really lifted the roof had that gone in.'

'Yeah, I really thought I had it.'

'Of course, we both know it can't continue.'

'What do you mean?'

'We both know your legs have gone and that you're going to start playing absolutely shit.'

'No, they haven't.'

'Oh, come on, Tony, how long have we been having these conversations? McCarthy will have you off in a minute. I can see Dave Connolly warming up as we speak.'

'No, not tonight. I'm going for the record. I'm going out with a bang.'

'A bang! Dear oh dear . . . when's the last time you made a bang for Ireland, Tony? How long is it since you've scored an international goal?'

'I know but . . .'

'Let me remind you: October 1997.'

'OK, but this is my last game at Lansdowne Road. I owe it to the people of Ireland to run my legs into the ground.'

'The people of Ireland. Don't make me laugh! What would the people of Ireland think if they knew Theresa's secret?'

'Fuck off! You promised . . . We made a deal!'

'OK, but admit it, you are getting tired.'

'Just a bit.'

'You're playing in spasms.'

'It comes and goes.'

'And that never used to happen in the past, did it?'

'No, that's true. I used to be able to go for ninety minutes.'

'The Monaco game on Wednesday . . . the travel . . . your knee . . . it's starting to take its toll, isn't it?'

'It's been a tough week, all right.'

'And don't tell me you didn't notice the collective groan from the crowd when they heard you were replacing Niall!'

'Yes, now that you mention it, I did.'

'Admit it, mate, it was a terrible mistake to keep playing. The papers will murder you tomorrow. You should have bowed out gracefully with Andy and Ray Houghton two years ago.'

'Yeah, maybe you're right.'

Mick McCarthy calls me to the touchline after seventy-five minutes. The game finishes 1–1.

Chapter Three
Last Throw of the Dice

Do not go gentle into that good night,
Old age should burn and rave at close of day;
Rage, rage against the dying of the light.
– Dylan Thomas, 'Do not go gentle into that good night'

You cannot beat a good right hander.
– Lenny McLean, *The Guv'nor*

Although we damage our knees and bruise our toes and tear the odd muscle from time to time, nothing hurts as much in football as the truth. It's like being caught offside. On the morning after the drawn game with Turkey, there are linesmen with raised flags everywhere, highlighting what I have known deep down for some time. First there is a brief exchange between Mick McCarthy and Niall I happen to overhear – 'You've fucking got to be fit, Niall, we need you' – and then, the reviews in the morning papers:

The omens were not good when Ireland suffered a disastrous late withdrawal, when Niall Quinn cried off approaching kick-off time with a neck injury. His fitness will be monitored closely before Wednesday. He was replaced last night by Tony Cascarino, still a crowd favourite at Lansdowne Road, but nothing like as mobile or as effective as the Sunderland striker. Up against the determined Turkish number five, Ozalan Alpay, Cascarino failed to make much of an impression. *Sunday Tribune*

Cascarino: two moments in the first half apart, he was anonymous. Off the pace and unable to compete with the peerless Alpay in the air, he showed once more that his international career should have been ended long since. *Sunday Times*

Battled as hard as he could as a late replacement for the injured Niall Quinn but bar a first-half shot offered no threat to the Turks. Rating 7. *Ireland on Sunday*

Came in at the last minute when Niall Quinn's neck injury failed to clear up. Couldn't get enough power or direction on a Kilbane free but was later denied by a brilliant save when he connected with a Breen knockdown. Ran out of steam and could have been replaced earlier. Rating 5. *Sunday Independent*

The ratings always make me smile; I've had games where I've played well but got a 4 because I missed a couple of chances, and games where I've played poorly and got an 8 because I scored. Kevin Kilbane played really well last night but was given a 5 by one of the papers! Who judges these things? Stevie Wonder! And yet, while I would argue that my critics are unfair – they don't give me any credit for playing well in the first half and make no allowances for my week – I can't really argue with the bottom line: my time has gone.

The journey to the Turkish city of Bursa proves the mother of all transfers. Tired and crusty, we are hauled from our beds early for the four-hour flight to Istanbul, which is followed by a twenty-minute coach ride, a sixty-minute crossing of the Sea of Marmara and another eighty minutes by coach before we reach our hotel. On the final leg of the journey at Yalova, we encounter the first visible signs of the recent earthquake: mile after mile of displaced families, housed in makeshift plastic shacks by the side of the road. It's dark and raining outside and conditions look thoroughly miserable, but though we sympathize with their plight, our compassion is fleeting. One of the innate skills of the professional is his ability to identify what matters most in life and our thoughts immediately return to ourselves. And genuine causes for concern like: Will the journey ever end? Will the hotel be nice? Will the food be OK? Will we be able to use our mobile phones? Will the room have two double beds? And pay-per-view porn? And satellite TV?

Luckily, when eventually we arrive, the answer is yes to all of the above except the pay-per-view porn. The Kervansaray Termal Hotel is not exactly the Ritz, but it's fine.

The old firm game is scoreless with five minutes to play when John Collins wins the ball and sets off down the wing. Fifty thousand Celtic fans jump to their feet. They see Collins racing into Rangers territory. They see Tony Cascarino slipping his marker and breaking free. They see the winger cross the ball low to the striker's feet. They see a million-pound player in front of an open Rangers goal with a glorious opportunity at his feet . . .

They do not see the fear on my face at that moment. They do not hear the taunting of the little voice in my head. They have no idea that a ball played low across my body when I'm facing goal has always been my Achilles heel. They do not believe their eyes when I swipe frantically and completely miss the target. They do not feel compassion when I fall to my knees and cover my face in shame.

'You clumsy wanker!'

'I'm sorry.'

'You could have been a hero. It was all there in front of you, the winning of the game.'

'Yeah, I know.'

I jump to my feet and prepare to face the kick-off. Some strange things start happening. The players have stopped playing. The fever-pitch roar has suddenly dimmed. Every person in the ground is staring at me. I look to where my family are sitting in the stands. My mother is crying: 'He should never have left the hairdressing.' My son is shaking his head: 'You're not very good, Dad, are you?' My manager, Liam Brady, is being consoled on the bench by those who have managed me in the past.

'The lad needs help, Liam,' Graham Taylor says.

'*He's fucking crap,*' Jack Charlton blasts.

I walk towards them and begin to explain: 'Liam, I'm sorry. I've always had a thing about a ball played in low.' But the words have only just left my mouth when I am shaken by a screech and plunged into a world of almost total darkness. Heart thumping, I open my eyes and struggle to make sense of the sound and the shadows until a familiar face, unconscious in the bed alongside, brings it all into view. 'Shit! Niall! Bursa! I've been dreaming that dream again!' I glance at my watch and it is five o'clock in the morning. I roll over and listen until the strange, mournful chant of the call to prayer ends and I drift slowly back to sleep.

The day begins with a slow walk to the bathroom mirror, a long study of my reflection and the discovery of a fleck of grey in my hair. I wash and change and descend quickly to reception where, after securing a translation for brown, I slip discreetly out of the door in search of a chemist. It is time to start looking young again. Perception is everything in football. I remember, when I was just starting out at Gillingham, a story that appeared in the paper one day about a 25-year-old we had just signed from Fisher Athletic. Paul Shinners was another south Londoner and while I didn't know him personally, I did know he was older than twenty-five. A few weeks later, I put it to him one day when we were alone in the dressing room.

'Paul,' I said. 'I'm not being funny, but you're not twenty-five, are you?'

'No,' he laughed, 'I'm not.'

'How old are you, then?'

'I'm twenty-eight, but you can't come from non-league

football at twenty-eight now, can you? So I knocked three years off and no one has ever asked me to prove it.' It was a lesson that would serve me well. I've been dyeing my hair for as long as I can remember and make a point of presenting myself as smartly as possible when negotiating a contract. You wouldn't believe the difference a dye makes. Present yourself to the chairman in your naturally greying state and you're asking for trouble: 'Oh no, I'm not sure about this one. I don't think we'll get a year out of him.' But add a bit of colour to your roots and the contract is in the bag: 'Look at him, he's in great nick, I can't believe he's thirty-six! He must really look after himself.' It's just an illusion but the illusion works. In football, it's not what you are but what you appear to be that counts.

The colour costs four million Turkish lira, which seems a staggering amount to spend on your hair. I return to the hotel and after breakfast, slip upstairs and lock the door to the room. At a critical juncture of the process, there is a frantic rattle on the door. 'Open up, Cas,' Dave Connolly says, 'We're starting a game of cards.'

Colouring your hair is not a done thing in football; you can bleach it, or shave it, but the rest is taboo. 'Sorry, Dave, I'll be out in a minute,' I lie. 'I'm just having a bath.'

But Niall, who has just shaken himself from his nightly coma, immediately blows my cover. 'He's not in the bath at all,' he laughs. 'He's colouring his hair!'

Within seconds, the phone is buzzing and a queue has formed at the door – *'come out, you big poof!'* The ribbing continues at training and for the rest of the afternoon – a childish but welcome diversion in the on-going battle to stay sane.

A journalist, with whom I've been friendly for some time, invites me for coffee in the lobby after training. He is researching a feature for his paper and enquires about Mick and the mood in the camp. I offer the honest assessment that while the concession of a goal in Dublin is undoubtedly a setback, it is far from insurmountable and we all still believe we can

31

qualify. He makes a few notes and the interview ends. We order more coffee and chat about old times.

'This may seem an odd question, but what do you know about me?' I ask.

'I know you're a good player but not a great player,' he smiles, aping a well-known commentator.

'No, I'm serious. What do you know about me?'

'You're right, it is an odd question. What do I know about you? I know you're thirty-seven years old and Ireland's most capped player. I know you're a goal shy of the all-time scoring record. I know you've played in two World Cups and for Aston Villa, Celtic, Chelsea and Marseilles. I know you named your first son Michael after your Irish grandfather and your other son Teddy after Teddy Sheringham. I think you're possibly divorced but I'm not sure, and that you may have remarried a French girl but I'm not sure about that either. I know you're well liked by your peers and by the media. A typical streetwise cockney, I'd say; one of the nice guys.'

He crosses his legs and looks for a reaction. A favourite lyric comes to mind.

'But nice guys get washed away in the snow when the rain comes.'

He doesn't get it.

'Glen Campbell, "Rhinestone Cowboy".'

'Oh.'

'And is the rain coming?' he asks, after a pause.

'It's on its way,' I reply. 'This is my last season. I really can't see myself playing next year.'

'What are you going to do?'

'I don't know. I've a couple of small ideas but nothing sure.'

'What about a newspaper column?'

'Naah, I wouldn't be up to it. I don't suffer from amnesia.'

'What do you mean?'

'Well, in every paper you open these days there's an hysterical ex-professional preaching that "such and such should have scored this" and, "so and so should have done that," conveniently forgetting that when he played the game, he did exactly the same.'

He smiles and reaches for his cup but says nothing. It's time to let him know what's on my mind.

'I've been thinking about writing a book. What do you think?'

'There's a lot of them about,' he says. 'It depends on what you've got to say and why you want to say it.'

'How do you mean?'

'The bookshops are heaving with ex-footballers' tales. If you're thinking of it in terms of a pension, forget it. Publishers are the only people making money from books these days, unless your name is Alex Ferguson or you're married to a Spice Girl.'

'No, it wouldn't be for the money.'

'So why do you want to do it? Didn't you just mention something about players with short memories?

'Yeah, but it wouldn't be that kind of book. I'm not interested in talking about the games I've played or the goals I've scored or the wankers I've met in dressing rooms. I'm not interested in hurting anyone but myself.'

'And why would you want to hurt yourself?'

'Because I've made mistakes and hurt my two boys. Because a lot of things happened that they don't know or understand. Because there's more to football than the ninety minutes of a game and more to the people that play it than a 5 in the ratings. Because after eighteen years of being cheered and jeered and analysed, I would like people to know who I am.'

He folds his arms and rubs his chin and explains about a publisher he knows in London and asks me to wait while he gives her a call. When he returns, I am surprisingly anxious.

'Well, what did she say?'

'Would you like her exact words?'

'Go on.'

'She said, "No disrespect, but he's not exactly David Beckham."'

'Did she really?'

'Well, no, not exactly, but that was the gist of it. I'm sorry, Cas, but I can see where she's coming from – it's a hard one to sell. You're just not sexy enough.'

I nod and consider returning to my room but the urge to keep pushing is too strong. 'And what if, say, the book revealed something that was front-page news? Would that be sexy enough?'

'It might. What are we talking about?'

'Off the record?'

'Off the record.'

'What if Ireland's most capped international player wasn't *ever* qualified to play for Ireland?'

'You're not serious?'

'It depends what you mean by serious. Do I qualify to play for the Republic of Ireland? No. Am I prepared to go on the record? Yes. But it's not my only reason for doing a book and I'm not the only person to be considered here. There are a couple of important details that still have to be sorted.'

'What sort of details?'

'I can't say anything more for the moment.'

'Who else knows?'

'Andy Townsend . . . Niall . . . a small group of friends.'

'Fuck! That's unbelievable! Does it have to be a book? What about a double-page spread in a respectable Sunday newspaper?'

'Sorry, not interested.'

'OK, leave it with me,' he says.

We shake hands and agree to meet soon. He scurries back to the lobby like a dog with two tails.

What sort of a place is Bursa? I have absolutely no idea. It's like Zagreb and Vienna and Seville and Rome and all the other magnificent cities we have visited but never seen over the years. It's a hotel room with a ceiling and four walls; a four-day stretch in a prison without bars, where the wardens are friendly and the food is OK and the boredom is agony. What sort of day was Tuesday? Exactly the same as Monday. The wailing starts; we wake up. The wailing stops; we fall asleep again. We eat and train and sleep and eat and train and sleep until finally, at last, Wednesday brings the chance to escape . . .

I have always liked Niall Quinn. I first got to know him in the summer of '88, when we were bit players on an Ireland team that travelled to Germany for the European Championships. I remember in particular the second game of the tournament against the Soviet Union. We were both on the bench when the Soviets equalised, late in the second half, and Jack gave the order to warm up: 'Get ready Big Man!' Responding immediately, as you do when Jack gives an order, we jumped to our feet and started sprinting down the touchline when Jack completely lost the head: '*Not fucking you, Niall!*' It was one of the great put-downs. He was quite shy and timid back then but has changed out of all recognition since. He's a character now, one of the leaders on the team, and although our rivalry has always been intense we've never allowed it to cloud our friendship. The thing I appreciate most about him is his sincerity when he wishes you the best. He is not two-faced like many in the game. He has always wanted me to do well for Ireland, as I have him, and there have been times when we've felt guilty about taking the other's place. 'See you in an hour' is our standing joke before kick-off; when he's called in, I'm sent out – or at least that's how it used to be.

On the morning of the game, I inform him of my decision to retire, come what may. 'Don't be stupid,' he says. 'What if we qualify? Stay in there. We'll need you next summer.' For once, I know he's lying. For once, I don't mind.

We lunch at 12.30 a.m. and play cards for an hour. Niall has declared himself fit to play and as a result, I spend a worry-free afternoon having my hair cut (another four million!) and killing time with the book I am reading by Lenny McLean entitled *The Guv'nor*. In Chapter Five, the infamous prize

fighter has just been hired to 'mind' a demolition man called
Fred . . .

Next morning, I tucked myself in the caravan they used as
an office and I sat drinking coffee, having a smoke and
keeping an eye on the gates. A tipper lorry pulled in and this
big fella jumped down, all boots and no fucking brains. I
watched him as he went over to Fred. They started arguing
and Fred got poked in the chest by this mug's finger. They
came over to the caravan and Fred said to him, 'My partner
wants a word.'

As he put one foot on the metal steps I chinned him.
Down he went like a bag of shit. But I picked him up and did
him again; four of them and he's unconscious. Once I start I
don't stop. He had blood coming out of his ears and nose, and
his forehead was split open. I was going to give him some
more but Fred grabbed my shirt and pulled me back.
'Enough, Len, enough, don't kill him.' So to get rid of some
steam, I picked up a lump of concrete and flung it through
the windscreen of his lorry. We brought him around, slung
him in the back of the tipper, and parked him two streets
away. Never saw him again.

I met Lenny McLean once at a car dealer's in Streatham. We
shook hands and it was like clutching a shovel; I gripped as
hard as possible but he crunched every finger in my hand. He
had just started acting and was quite full of himself but,
tempting as it was to call him a flash bastard, I decided to bite
my lip. The guy was an absolute maniac; he'd have crushed me
on the spot.

The night is fresh; the stadium is humming; the situation –
Turkey 0 Ireland 0 – is desperate. I sit in frustration watching
the stalemate until late in the second half, when Mick finally
gives the order to warm up. Alan McLaughlin, who is sitting to
my right, springs to his feet and follows the other substitutes

down the touchline. I delay a moment until they've cleared the bench, then charge past Mick, looking fiercely determined – an old trick I mastered under Jack when the lads used to joke that I'd pull every stroke in the book to get a game. Do they expect me to apologize? Anything goes when there are five subs on the bench and you are desperate to play. And I am desperate to play. In the eightieth minute, the moment I've been waiting for arrives. Mick orders me to get stripped, Jeff Kenna is called to the side and with nine minutes left, I run on to the pitch for my eighty-eighth and final appearance in green. Strangely, I feel little emotion as I race into position; no tinge of sadness that a huge chapter of my life is about to end. My thoughts are dominated by the notion of making a difference. I want a goal to be my encore, to exit the stage in a blaze of glory, to be remembered as having delivered when it mattered. Pathetic, isn't it? As if eighteen years wouldn't teach a man something about Roy of the Rovers endings . . .

The final minutes of the game flash like seconds. Six are added for injuries and stoppages and though I reach and stretch and strain every sinew, nothing drops for me or for the team. When the final whistle blows, ecstatic Turkish players and officials come swarming on to the pitch, but for me, there is only the painful sting of failure and the seething frustration that losing always brings.

Sore and edgy, I turn and begin walking towards the tunnel, but the number two has raced across to cut me off. He's sneering and mouthing triumphantly. Winning is not enough. He wants to rub my nose in it. Instinctively, I flick out my foot and watch as he trips and regains his balance. Instinctively, he swings his arm and catches me with a sledgehammer blow to the jaw. Stunned, but rather pleased to be still standing, I lash back immediately but am pounded and walloped from all sides as more players arrive and an ugly brawl ensues. Tony Hickey arrives and shepherds me to the safety of the dressing room. I am already feeling guilty . . .

Mick Byrne arrives with some ice for my swollen lip. I

shower and change and tour the dressing room, commiserating with my younger team mates. Mick McCarthy is changing in the adjoining dressing room.

'I think you know what's coming,' I announce.

'I've a fair idea,' he says.

'I was going to call it a day even if we qualified.'

'Yeah? Well, thanks for everything, Cas. You've been brilliant for me.'

We sit in silence, wrapped in our own thoughts, on the marathon transfer by coach and boat back to Istanbul. I take my final Irish jersey out of a bag and send it around the coach to be signed. It comes back and I gaze at the squiggles, trying to figure them out. I've known Mick McCarthy and Mick Byrne since 1985 and little Charlie O'Leary almost as long; Niall Quinn, Denis Irwin, Roy Keane, Alan Kelly, Alan Mac – we've had some good times together, some of the best of my life. We reach the airport in the early hours and in the confusion go our separate ways without saying farewell. They're heading for Dublin, and onward connections to England. I'm heading for Frankfurt, and an onward connection to France. One chapter ends, another continues. That's football. That's life.

The flight from Istanbul to Frankfurt touches down at 8.15 a.m. The police are waiting and check every passport as we step from the plane. In the delay, I am lucky to make my connecting flight to Luxemburg. I pick up my car at the long-term car park and drive to Nancy, arriving just in time for lunch with Virginia and Maeva. It is Thursday, 18 November. My international career has ended. I am happy to be home.

Chapter Four
Ten Days in November

We all run on two clocks. One is the outside clock, which ticks away our decades and brings us ceaselessly to the dry season. The other is the inside clock, where you are your own timekeeper and determine your own chronology, your own internal weather and your own rate of living. Sometimes the inner clock runs itself out long before the outer one, and you see a dead man going through the motions of living.

– Max Lerner

Friday, 19 November 1999
All over the world, in London and Paris and New York and Rome, millions of people jumped out of bed this morning thinking, 'Thank God it's Friday.' Not at 6 avenue de la Garenne, they didn't; not *chez moi*. After spending a wonderfully relaxing evening with Virginia, eating fine food and drinking fine wine and doing, well, too much of what professional athletes are supposed to do in moderation, the only thought in my head when I opened my eyes was, 'Shit, here I go again.' I did not want to be Tony Cascarino. I did not want to be a star with Nancy FC. I did not want to be a professional footballer. I felt physically, mentally and emotionally drained and woke up this morning feeling nothing but contempt for the game.

After leaving Maeva at school, I had a long soak in the bath and spent the morning trying to shake off the emptiness that has clung to me since Bursa. The club called just before lunchtime. Experience teaches you nothing. You always hope for the best. I wanted them to say: 'Tony, you've played three games in seven days; spend the weekend at home with your family and we'll see you next week.' They said: 'Tony, training today at *quinze heures trente*. Be prepared to leave immediately afterwards for Nantes.'

Virginia wasn't impressed. 'Call them back,' she said, 'and tell them you're sick. I mean, look at you! You *are* sick! You're covered in bruises from head to toe!'

Sorely tempted, I considered it for a moment but decided to report for duty and just get on with it, but I should probably, in hindsight, have stayed at home. At my age, 'just getting on with it' is never enough.

Most of the lads had seen 'the fight' on Eurosport and I was subjected to a right ribbing in the dressing room when I arrived at Forêt de Haye. We trained for an hour and then had a meeting with the club president, Monsieur Rousselot, who announced a £3000-per-man bonus if we can beat Nantes. Normally, our *'prime de victoire'* is £1000, but because Nantes are *'une équipe directe'* – direct as in direct rivals because we're both in the shit at the bottom of the table – he announced a triple prime. When the meeting was over, we drove our cars to the regional airport at Epinal and flew to Nantes in one of those awful, twenty-seater private jets that never seem properly maintained and always seem to have accidents. The freezing cold weather delayed our departure for hours and it was well after midnight when we eventually arrived at the Hôtel Mercure.

Tonight, I'm rooming with Cedric Lecluse, a 26-year-old defender who phones home at least twenty times a day and is more besotted by his wife than any man I've ever known. The love story began when they were both teenagers. Cedric was an apprentice footballer at Nancy. Sylvie was a check-out girl at the local supermarket. Every day, several times a day, Cedric would queue up with an apple or a Perrier or some chocolate until she finally agreed to a date. He's been totally devoted to her ever since. There's a decency and innocence about Cedric that's really refreshing but he is also incredibly naïve. He has told me things about his life I wouldn't tell my closest friend – never mind a footballer I happened to be sharing a room with! I can't imagine him in an English dressing room. He'd be absolutely destroyed.

Saturday, 20 November
Nantes 2, Nancy 0.

'Well, what can I say, even by your own unique standards, that was abysmal!'

'Yeah, I just couldn't shake myself.'

'So what's the excuse this time?'

'I don't have any.'

'Can't wait to see the ratings in L'Equipe *tomorrow morning?'*

'I'm not interested.'

'No, that was patently obvious.'

Woke up this morning feeling like Niall Quinn: I couldn't get out of bed for the traditional morning warm-up, and spent the entire afternoon in a coma when I went back to it after lunch. It was payback time for the sleepless night and long journey home from Bursa. When I pushed back the sheets, I felt absolutely wrecked. And it showed. Because of my experience, and the fact that I'm one of only two internationals at Nancy, the manager usually says nothing to me in the dressing room before a game. Tonight it was, *'Tony, un mot, enthousiasme.'* I must have had 'Do not disturb' written all over me! Even the president picked it up.

'Ça va, Tony?' he enquired, as I was walking down the tunnel to warm up.

'Oui, ça va bien,' I replied.

I should have said, *'Non, Monsieur Rousselot, ça ne va pas du tout.'* I should have said, 'To be perfectly honest Monsieur Rousselot, I feel absolutely fucked.' But he's an honourable man, our president, and has always treated me well, so I told him what he wanted to hear: *'Oui, ça va bien.'*

And tonight we paid the price. My game is all about one-to-one combat: I'm at my best when I forget the team stuff and reduce the ninety minutes to an individual battle between myself and whoever picks me up. Tonight, I threw the towel in from the kick-off. I did not contest my battle. I did not contribute to the team. I spent the whole game wishing I was somewhere else. I was absolutely shite. When it was over, I couldn't wait to get out of the dressing room and back to the airport, and tonight I'm feeling as low as I have been since coming to France: I'm sick of the team and sick of the game and sick of everything about the life. On the rent-a-jet ride home, I actually wanted the thing to crash.

Virginia was sleeping when I got back to the apartment. I made a cup of tea and sat down to watch the blue channel, *XXL*, which I occasionally do when I'm alone and feeling bad. Two dwarfs, dressed as garden gnomes, were ripping each other's waistcoats off and about to start humping on a lawn.

'*For fuck's sake, Tony, you're not feeling that bad!*'

'*No, you're right, I'm not.*'

Disgusted, I reached for the zapper and marched limply off to bed.

Sunday, 21 November
This morning I had it all worked out. 'I'm going to see the president tomorrow,' I announced to Virginia.

'For what?' she asked.

'To see if he'll offer me a deal to terminate my contract.'

'Don't be stupid! It's only one bad game. Next week you play Marseilles. Don't tell me you don't want to play against Marseilles?'

'No, I'm sick of it. I've had enough. Rousselot will understand when I explain. He won't want to pay me to the end of the season if he knows I don't want to play. It would suit us both to negotiate a settlement.'

'Well, you know I'm with you whatever you decide, but I think you've got no chance.'

'Why not?'

'Think about it, Tony. You're Nancy's top scorer! Their most experienced player! He'd be mad to let you walk away.'

'Not after the way I played last night.'

'Forget about last night. You were tired. It was a *jour sans*. Everybody has a *jour sans*.'

It was good to talk. As the day wore on, my depression began to lift and after a lovely lunch we went out shopping for furniture this afternoon and bought a new Indonesian bed. I like spending money, particularly when I'm down; I'm like some of those serial women shoppers you read about, who keep buying clothes when depressed. I spent the evening chatting on the phone to family and friends. I've been blessed with some really good friends. Chris McCarthy, who I've known since childhood, and Steve Wishart, who was my manager at Crockenhill, called with all the latest from London. And I phoned Andy Townsend.

'Thought you might call,' he said.

'How's that?' I asked.

'Well, it's Sunday, isn't it? You always call cheap rate.'

Andy is always at least a forty-five-minute conversation and was laughing about the fight in Turkey. 'That is so typical of you,' he said. 'You were exactly the same when we lost in Belgium [World Cup qualifying playoff] in '97!'

L'Equipe gave me a 4.5 (out of ten) this morning, which is pretty poor but accurate for once. I'm trying to put the game out of my head. Virginia's right – a *jour sans*.

Monday, 22 November
Our manager, Laszlo Boloni, has never had a *jour sans*. Casually mention you're tired at training and he immediately doubles the workload. Laszlo doesn't believe in being tired. Tiredness is a state of mind. Tiredness is an excuse. And Laszlo never makes excuses. 'The difference between winning and losing,' he says, 'is physical and mental strength.' A former

Rumanian international, and one of the great defenders of his generation, he played on the Steau Bucharest team that beat Barcelona in the European Cup Final in 1986. That they won the game's greatest prize on penalties after 120 minutes of stalemate would have made it extra special for Laszlo. He would have thought, 'Fuck the beautiful game! We won! We did them! Winning is what counts.' Laszlo has always seen football as a game of chess.

He is, without doubt, one of the most interesting men I've ever met. And easily the most superstitious. Three years ago, shortly after I'd joined from Marseilles, I was having dinner with the team one evening before a game, when a team-mate pointed to the clock on the wall. 'It's five minutes past eight,' he said. 'I'll bet you anything you want, that in exactly three minutes' time, Laszlo Boloni will walk through that door.' And sure enough, at exactly eight minutes past eight, we were joined by the manager. A week later, on the eve of our next game, I was making my way to the restaurant after being slightly delayed by a call when I happened upon the manager, fidgeting in the corridor outside. I looked at my watch and it was six minutes past eight. Two minutes later, Laszlo entered the room.

The Novotel chain runs two hotels in Nancy: the Novotel Laxou, a three-minute drive from the training ground, and the Novotel Houdemont, twenty minutes further to the south. Last year, after a string of bad results, Laszlo decided to switch the team hotel from the Laxou to the Houdemont and was immediately rewarded with a change in fortune. We continued to use the Houdemont for the next few games until the visit of Monaco, when we were forced to return to the Laxou because Monaco had booked the Houdemont months in advance. Laszlo wasn't pleased. On the morning after the game, he stormed down to the Houdemont and block-booked the hotel for the rest of the season. And for the following season as well.

This morning, there were two cast-iron certainties when I got to the training ground: one, that his rusty white Citroën would have already arrived and two, that it would be parked in the first space to the left of the clubhouse entrance. The reason I was sure he'd take the old Citroën to work was because he used his Mercedes last week and always switches when we're beaten. And the reason I knew he'd park to the left of the clubhouse was because he parked in front of it last week. His obsession knows no bounds. During games, we are forbidden from asking the referee the time or from glancing at the stadium clock. 'You should be concentrating on the game!' he says. 'I want 110 per cent right to the end!' And he goes absolutely crazy if we sing or whistle in the dressing room – apparently, in Rumania, it brings bad luck.

He seemed unusually distant this morning at training and worked us very hard. Normally after a game, he calls me over and asks my opinion but this morning there was just a perfunctory shake-of-hands and a slightly gruff *'bonjour'*. He'd obviously spent the weekend reviewing my performance against Nantes. We've always had a good relationship and I feel guilty for letting him down but there's no point in explaining I was tired.

Tuesday, 23 November
I called Sarah in London this evening. When phoning my ex-wife, I use the kitchen phone rather than one in the hall because I can close the door behind me and it reduces the chance of Maeva being heard. It's not that I'm ashamed of her or anything but if the roles had been reversed, and my wife had run off and had a daughter by another man, I know it would upset me to hear her voice in the background, so I try to be as sensitive as possible when phoning from home. As it turned out, I needn't have bothered: Sarah was out and had left a baby-sitter, so I was saved our usual brief and frosty exchange . . .

I phone the boys two or three times a week. They are complete opposites: Michael is ten and a computer game wizard; Teddy is seven and loves football. Since the divorce, it's hard to get Teddy to talk normally on the phone. He'll come on and make these silly animal noises and won't say a word unless he's scored a goal and I mention football. That he was first to the phone this evening was unusual.

'Michael is upstairs in bed,' he explained. 'He has a stomach ache.'

'Yeah? And how are you doing, Ted?'

'Fine. We played on Sunday and won 1–0. Mummy said I played well but Grandad said I didn't.'

'Never mind, Mummy is always right. I'm sure you were brilliant.'

When the conversation ended and I had spoken briefly to Michael, I was torn for the rest of the evening with the guilt that has afflicted me regularly since I walked out of their lives.

Sometimes, when it really gets me down, I retreat into a shell and won't say a word for hours. At first, these mood swings caused friction with Virginia, who believed I was blaming the loss of my sons on her. And sometimes I was . . . well, it's human nature, isn't it? You blame everyone except yourself. Lately, we have both been coping much better. 'Why don't you phone the boys?' she says, whenever I go quiet. And though talking to them is not the same as being with them, for the moment it's the best I can do. They stay with us whenever there's a break in school and holiday with us in summer and (to Sarah's credit) get on really well with Maeva. The day may come when they point the finger at Virginia – 'She's not my mother!' – or stand up and pass judgement – 'I'm not having my Dad do what you did!' – but hopefully I'll have finished playing by then and be back in England and we'll be closer.

Wednesday, 24 November

A journalist called at the training ground this afternoon and asked my opinion on the latest from Marseilles. Another called this evening looking for the same. The latest from Marseilles is that they've just sacked their manager, Raymond Courbis, and replaced him with Bernard Casoni, a former team mate of mine. And because I once played at Marseilles, and played with

Bernard at Marseilles, and will play against Marseilles on Saturday in Bernard's first game in charge, I've become another angle on the story . . . except that I'm not at all sure Laszlo will name me in the side. We trained twice today, a hard, physical session in the morning and a keep-ball session and some pattern play in the afternoon. You can always read the way a manager is thinking from the sides he plays during the week. I played up front for the kids this afternoon against a team with most of the regulars. You'd have to have been blind not to spot the odd man out. I thought, 'He's weighing up his options here – he's thinking about leaving you out.' And drove home feeling strangely disappointed. Of all the teams we will play this season, there is none I look forward to more than Marseilles.

Steve Staunton, the second most capped player ever to play for the Republic of Ireland, also called this evening, with confirmation that the Football Association of Ireland have granted us a joint testimonial at Lansdowne Road in May. Steve, or Stan as he has always been known, has agreed a deal with Liverpool for the game and thinks he'll be able to convince Robbie Fowler and Michael Owen to play, which should draw a crowd. I joked that I wasn't sure I'd make it that far. May seems an eternity away.

Thursday, 25 November
I picked up Laurent for training this morning. Laurent is Laurent Moracchini, a 32-year-old Corsican who idolizes Roy Keane and who was once banned for six months for head-butting a player at Monaco. He's one of the world's great pessimists – we are less than halfway through the season but he's convinced we're going down. I collect Laurent for training most days, mainly because he's my best mate on the team but also because it allows him to leave his wife the car. That's the reality of life as a professional with Nancy; although we play in the French Premier division, there's no comparison with the Premiership in England. *France Football* published an article recently comparing average salaries in the two premier

leagues, showing that players in England earn three times more than those in France. And pay much less tax! In France, teams can't chop and change players as they can in England. Here, you start the season with a squad and, regardless of injuries, are only allowed to buy one extra player between the opening game and the mid-season *trêve* or break at Christmas. And then just one more player between *la trêve* and the end of the season. Every club has a budget to which it must adhere rigorously. If Nancy is relegated this season, everyone at the club – from the highest paid player and the manager to the coaching and administrative staff – will automatically have a 20 per cent wage cut for next season – a measure imposed by the French Football Federation to stop clubs going bust. So you can understand why I wasn't exactly flavour of the month with the secretaries and cleaners after my performance on Saturday. We lose, they lose; we get a cut, they get a cut. We're all in the same boat. And already sunk, according to Laurent . . .

Friday, 26 November
After training in the afternoon we had a team meeting with Laszlo, at which I was reminded again how much ball I had lost against Nantes (*'There isn't a chance he's going to play you tomorrow night!'*). We then drove straight to the Houdemont where – because Cedric is suspended and Laurent smokes (that's the other thing about French football – in England the vice is alcohol but here it's cigarettes) – I am rooming with the infamous 'X'. One of the things that amazes me about Nancy is that, after six clubs and hundreds of team-mates, I should find myself at the end with three of the most unique people I've ever met. There's the mystery of Laszlo and his ongoing superstitions, the wonder of Cedric and his undying love for his wife and finally 'X', in some ways the most unique of all.

As with Laszlo and Cedric, there's a lot about 'X' I really admire: he's intelligent, speaks pretty good English and always tries to be a good pro. But there are other things about him I will never understand. He does not use shampoo. He does not use toothpaste. He does not use aftershave or deodorant. And he smells. The second time we roomed together I put a clothes peg in my bag and slipped it over my nose as I was getting into bed. He looked at me and sniffed his T-shirt: 'It's not me,' he said. 'I don't smell.'

'You fucking do,' I countered.

Nothing changed. It's not that he's allergic or objects to animal testing; he just doesn't believe in wasting money on soap or perfume. He is Europe's tightest, smelliest man. His thriftiness is manic. He has a mobile phone that can only receive calls and he always wears the club suit to weddings and functions. But that's just for starters. Once, we were rooming together and he said: 'Do you know you can eat for free?'

'What do you mean, "You can eat for free",' I scoffed. 'You have to buy food.'

'No,' he said. 'Check the labels the next time you shop; there's always a line that says that the customer can demand a refund if he isn't happy with the product.'

'But you still have to pay for the stamp,' I said. 'It will cost at least three francs to send it back.'

'Yes,' he agreed, 'but you don't do it for something that just costs a couple of francs, you do it for something more expensive. Think about it. I'm telling you, you can basically eat for free.'

There was a pause as I tried to figure it out.

'And I suppose you pay your TV licence as well,' he said.

'Of course I do.'

'You're mad,' he said. 'You don't have to, you know.'

'What do you mean, "You don't have to"?'

'You can refuse entry. Legally, the inspectors are not entitled to enter your house.'

I laughed, but he was serious.

During pre-season training in Munster, we decided one night, during a session of cards, that we'd forego the evening meal and just send someone out for a McDonald's, or a 'Macdo' as we say in these parts. To the surprise of all, it was 'X' who generously volunteered. And then came the proviso. 'I'll go,' he said, 'but you've got to pay for my petrol and you've got to buy my Macdo.' There was uproar. Even by his own miserly standards it was a new low. After a great deal of negotiating, we agreed to buy his Macdo but refused to pay for the petrol. He wouldn't budge. We sent someone else. A week later, at the end of the training camp, we were presented with gift packs of pâté and cheese after playing one of the local teams. Most of the lads weren't bothered and discarded them in the dressing room. 'X' gathered everything up and took it home.

Tonight, I tackled him again on his frugality: 'You must,' I said, 'have some pleasures in life!'

'Of course I do,' he responded, surprised. 'I read books and watch films and . . .'

'Oh, so you spend money on books, then?'

'Well, no, my girlfriend is at university and she gets them from the library and passes them on.'

'But you watch films? You rent videos?'

'No, I wait until they're shown on Canal plus. It may take a year or two but you see them all, sooner or later.'

'And what about holidays? When's the last time you treated yourself to a good time abroad?'

'Abroad! Why would I want to go abroad? France is the most beautiful country in the world.'

As I say, unique.

Saturday, 27 November
Nancy 2, Marseilles 2

Laszlo announced the team at the final team meeting just before we left the hotel. It was a surprise and a delight to hear my name which, when I think about it now, doesn't make a great deal of sense, given that I despised the fucking game a week ago.

And to be fair, nothing has changed. I could happily abandon the game tomorrow; I moan and bitch and complain about it six days a week. But for as long as I'm involved, there will always be something about Saturday. From our first day to our last, we are all addicted to making the team.

In the dressing room I thought about changing my boots before the game. I hadn't scored in two attempts against Turkey or in the four games since my hat-trick against Rennes and always switch to a new pair when my goalless streak hits five. At the last minute, I changed my mind and decided to give them one more chance. Scored twice tonight and played great. What can I say except they obviously feared for their lives.

It has often been said that the joy of scoring goals is greater than sex but personally I'd compare it more with masturbation. I've always found sex to be an absolute pleasure, but scoring goals has only ever brought relief. My first tonight, after fifty-one minutes, was a classic example of what I've always done best; Laurent did well and played in a great cross and I beat the defender and headed into the net. The second, however, was slightly more difficult. Marseilles hit back, with two goals in two minutes, after we had opened the scoring and looked set to cruise to victory, until the seventy-first minute when we were awarded a penalty. I've taken all our penalty kicks this season and have scored each time, but the goal is always that bit narrower when your team is trailing. Feeling terribly nervous when I placed the ball on the spot, I just couldn't make up my mind . . .

'Do what you always do, blast it.'

'Don't be ridiculous! You've played with these guys! He'll know exactly what you always do!'

'OK, place it right.'

'No, I fancy hitting it left.'

'OK, hit it left.'

'No, maybe you're right.'

'HIT THE FUCKING THING!'

I placed it to the right and scored.

Two-two was a good result in the circumstances (Marseilles missed a last-minute penalty) and a great result for me. When it was over, and I walked towards the dressing room, I couldn't help but wonder what the fanatical Marseilles fans would be thinking. Since being sold off to Nancy, I have scored more goals per season than any of the star names bought to replace me – a fact that I had just underlined again. I was hoping they were thinking, 'We pay £3m for [Christophe] Dugarry, £5m for [Fabrizio] Ravenelli and allow a player who scores more than both, to walk away for nothing!' I was hoping they were thinking, 'Why the fuck did we let him go?' Monsieur Rousselot seemed pleased in the dressing room. Laszlo nodded and slapped me on the back. I sat down and kicked off my boots and enjoyed the moment. Better than sex? No. Just relief that I'd done my job.

Sunday, 28 November

At my age, whenever you get on a run of two or three games without scoring, you are always 'finished'; it is always 'the End'. I've reached 'the End' a few times during these last two seasons but always managed to secure a stay of execution with a timely goal. It's often said that you are only as good as your last game but in my experience, this doesn't really apply until you reach your mid-thirties. Although I'm thirty-seven years old, I am consistently a much better player than I was at twenty-seven. I train harder; I rest more; I watch what I eat. Why? Because I don't have an option. I am three bad performances from the End.

When I was younger I used to get away with murder. I remember, at Gillingham, my season ended in February one year when I picked up a knee injury. I didn't play for three months and then went on holiday to Tenerife with Sarah in June. Aware on my return to London that I'd put on a couple of pounds, I decided to weigh myself on a public scales at Paddington station. It was the night of the Bruno–Witherspoon fight and I'd just read in the paper that Bruno had tipped the scales at 16 st. 2 lb. When I stood on the scales I was exactly 1lb lighter than him! Two stone overweight, I should have been distraught, but the 'the End' wasn't a problem back then and I just laughed it off and shrugged my shoulders: 'Hey, I could fight tonight!'

I got some good reviews in the local papers this morning and spent the day feeling good about myself. Tomorrow, we resume training for our next game against Sedan. Saturday will count for nothing as we go back to the drawing board and I'll be three games away once again from the End. But strangely, tonight, it feels more like the beginning.

All over the world, in London and Paris and New York and Rome, millions of people are going to bed tonight thinking, 'Oh fuck, tomorrow's Monday.' Not at 6 avenue de la Garenne they're not. Not *chez moi*. The dark clouds of a week ago seem a distant memory now. Suddenly, the game feels wonderful again, just like it did at the start . . .

Chapter Five
The Dominic Effect

Part of the reason for the ugliness of adults, in a child's eyes, is that the child is usually looking upwards, and few faces are at their best when seen from below.

– George Orwell, 'Such, Such were the Joys'

People react to fear, not love – they don't teach that in Sunday School, but it's true.

– Richard Nixon

A little boy lies on his bed with his radio in the summer of '76. It's the first Tuesday in May and the battle for the league championship has gone to the wire. To retain their title, and deny season-long-rivals Queens Park Rangers an historic first championship triumph, Liverpool must win or draw with Wolves in the final game of the season. To avoid relegation and a return to Division Two, Wolves must beat Liverpool. The little boy listens as the excitement builds at Molineux. Posters of Kevin Keegan and Steve Heighway and John Toshack adorn his bedroom wall. The boy also likes Millwall but there is no team quite like Liverpool. And no player like Kevin Keegan he would more like to be.

The game kicks off. Steve Kindon gives the home side the perfect start with a goal after thirteen minutes. Ray Kennedy almost equalizes, but his volley is just tipped over. Half-time comes and goes. The little boy wriggles and wrestles with the sheets. After fifty-five minutes Jimmy Case is called to the touchline and David Fairclough runs on. Supersub! Ten

54

minutes pass. An upset is on the cards. Liverpool on the attack. Just fifteen minutes left. The ball is pumped forward to Toshack. He rises and backheads it on. Keegan has made a run on the blind side . . . *Kevin Keegan scores!* The little boy jumps from his bed with delight.

The little boy's name is Tony Cascarino. His little home at 10 Garden Cottages is in St Paul's Cray, near Orpington, Kent. The little snapshot of his childhood is one of many happy memories he has presented to reporters and writers over the years. Would he have offered more of the same to Graham Taylor's sports psychologist? Probably. Why? Because that's what footballers do these days. We drive flash cars and wear flash clothes and behave like flash pop stars; and we shape and mould the truth about our lives and present ourselves as shiny, happy people in the pages of *Hello* . . .

I was twelve years old when I discovered what it is to be afraid. It happened on a cold afternoon in December when I was walking home to 10 Garden Cottages with my best friend Chris McCarthy. Christmas was coming and for weeks we had been working on a plan to make money from our fellow pupils at St Joseph's Secondary School. First we had compiled a shopping list of the things they most wanted for Christmas. Then today we had taken the bus to Orpington and nicked what was required. It was a no-lose situation. By selling the order at seriously reduced prices we were guaranteed a nice little earner. Delighted with a job well done, we had stashed the loot into two large plastic bags and had just started the climb at the bottom of our road when we happened to bump into my parents. Not part of the plan. My heart skipped a beat and I decided to bluff it out.

'Hi, Mum. Hi, Dad. Where're you off to, then?'

Mum smiled. My father – no great surprise – was his usual crusty self.

'What's in the bags?' he snapped.

'Err . . . nothing.' I panicked.

It wasn't very convincing. My father took one of the bags and opened it and, without saying a word, handed it to Mum. The punch came from nowhere and spun me across the path. Stunned, I tried to find my bearings and catch a breath but everything was moving. A neighbour, Mr Choules, was staring across from his driveway in disbelief. Still shaking, I struggled to my feet and he hit me again. He thumped me as a man would thump another man. He booted and bombed me with every ounce of his strength for a hundred yards until we reached our house. Mum was pleading with him to stop but the battery didn't end until I reached my bedroom. Mum was worried that I was seriously hurt and sat with me for hours. I had lumps and bruises everywhere and ached all over as I lay on the bed but more acute than the pain was the stinging sensation of damp between my legs: I had wet myself.

My mother had the world at her feet on that warm summer's evening in 1959. She was sixteen years old, had just found a job in London and was waiting for her boyfriend outside the Rose Croft Social Club in St Paul's Cray, when fate smiled and gave her a wink: 'Ain't he turned up yet?' She had never met Dominic Cascarino before and wasn't sure she wanted to. 'Don't worry,' she replied coolly. 'He will.' A week later she noticed him again at the dance in the social club. Three years older and a fluent Italian speaker, he told her he lived in London and had taken the train out with some friends.

She thought a bit more of him, second time around: Dominic was witty, smart and 'different' because he came from the city. They danced and made a date to do it again. They dated again and before the end of the summer, my mother was pregnant. They married as quickly as arrangements could be made and moved in with my mother's parents, Michael and Agnes O'Malley. It wasn't an ideal start to wedded life. My grandfather wasn't, for obvious reasons, that keen on his new son-in-law, but they made the best of it for a year until my parents found a place of their own. My sister,

Mandy, was born in February 1960 and the family was completed, two years later on 1 September, when my mother gave birth to a son. My life had begun.

We choose our friends, not our family. I never chose my Dad. My first tangible memory of him was a severe smacking when I was six or seven years old. I'm not sure what I did to deserve it, but then it never took much. My father was a crusty man with a volatile temper and he was almost always in a bad mood. As a boy, I didn't understand what bad moods were, but the knack of bringing out the worst in him seemed to come naturally. From the day I was born there seemed to be a chasm between us that widened the closer I became to my mother. I adored my mother and followed her constantly around the house as a boy but would never sit alone in the same room as a father who never hugged or kissed or showed me any affection. He wanted me to be like Mandy, spirited and fiery and confrontational, to be an Italian, a true Cascarino; but I just didn't have the testosterone. I was timid and docile and more an O'Malley by nature. A dreaded mummy's boy.

When I was nine, he came to watch me playing football at school one afternoon. We were hammered 7–2 and he did nothing but shout at me all through the game. It was miserable. I could see all the other parents looking at him and towards the end I completely lost it and told him to give me a break. He brought me home and gave me a beating. He swore he would never come to watch me again and as ever was as good as his word. The experience left me physically and mentally scarred. The bruises quickly healed but the emotional wounds lingered. I performed poorly in school and generally lacked confidence. I wet the bed until I was fourteen years old.

The eruptions continued through my teenage years. I had a habit of lying on the carpet in front of the fire that used to really get up his nose. Incensed that I was 'blocking the heat for everyone else', he'd lash out with his boot and kick me in the back. One night, a few months after my seventeenth birthday, he did it for the last time. I'd spent the day labouring on a building site and had collapsed on the carpet in front of the TV. My father had also had a hard day and returned home even later.

'Get your arse away from the fire,' he roared.

'No, I'm not getting up,' I replied, instinctively.

It wasn't planned. The words had already left my mouth when I realized I'd rebelled.

I closed my eyes and braced myself for the inevitable.

Nothing if not consistent, he jumped off the sofa and hoofed me in the ribs: 'I'm not going to tell you again, get your arse away from the fire.'

Gasping as the air was toe-poked from my lungs, I coughed and spluttered and decided to hold my ground: 'No, not this time.'

Enraged, he picked up a glass and flung it across the room. It shattered and stuck in my hand as I lifted my arm to protect myself.

It would be easy to describe what happened next as that classic scene from the movies where the coward of the county breaks and shows the world he's a real man by unleashing seventeen years of pent-up fury on the bastard who has cruelly abused him. But it wasn't like that. It wasn't like that at all. With blood gushing from my hand, I crossed the room to face him. We stood eye to eye and without saying a word, both understood he would never hit me again. And it was strange, but I felt no sense of joy or elation when it was over and the moment had passed. Just a sadness I couldn't fathom. Just an awful nagging guilt that gnawed away at me for days.

There was one port of refuge from the violent storms. Don and Molly Wilson lived next door but were always more than neighbours. I remember one night in particular, when my father went berserk and smashed everything in the kitchen. Mandy and I were ushered out of the house and we fled to the bunker next door. It was extremely embarrassing for my mother, but the Wilsons were very understanding and kind. I'm not sure what they made of my father. When you didn't know him, he could appear smart, witty and engaging, and it wouldn't be an act. Sometimes, when he was in good form, I'd look at him and think: 'Why can't you be like this at home? Why can't you be like this all the time?' The answer was that he couldn't help it. He was classic Jekyll and Hyde.

In the summer of 1971, he packed us off to Italy on holiday to visit our ancestral home. We travelled south to Rome and on to Monte Cassino (famed for its monastery and epic battle during the Second World War) and spent a week visiting relatives I had never met before and couldn't understand. My paternal grandparents, Dominic and Rosie Cascarino, were born in Monte Cassino and undoubtedly would have died there but for the war, when they fled to Scotland and settled in Edinburgh. My father was the first of eight children born there. Dominic Cascarino was a cobbler by trade but decided to open an ice-cream parlour for this new chapter in their lives. It didn't work. Edinburgh wasn't Naples. After seven years of struggling to survive, they moved south to London in search of better times.

Dominic and Rosie were a mystery to me. The only time they ever came to St Paul's Cray was on the day my parents were married. They never visited us at home or sent cards or presents on our birthday or conferred any of the warmth that flowed from the O'Malleys. They lived in a flat in Elephant and Castle in London and sometimes my father would take us up on the train to see them. Sunday was always a good day to visit because his brothers and sisters called and they'd gather around the table for cards. Except for Rosie. My grandmother never played. And never entered the room without permission. My grandfather treated her incredibly harshly. She'd come in, serve his tea and be dismissed like a dog to the kitchen: *'Vaffanoculo!'* And every time, she'd withdraw without a word.

The card games were amazing. My grandfather would

shuffle at the top of the table, smiling at the head of his big, happy family, until the money went down, when they'd start ripping each other apart. My grandfather hated losing and played each game as if he was playing for his life. I remember once casually glancing at his hand as I slowly toured the table. Furious, he threw his cards into the air and accused my father of using me to cheat. The game was abandoned, the table was upended and within seconds they were at each other's throats . . . just another typical Sunday with *la famiglia*. I'd sit and watch and listen to them squabble, and another piece of the puzzle that was my father, would fall into place. The anger that consumed him in my childhood was born in that flat at Elephant and Castle, a place where love and affection was as scarce as bread on the table and education a luxury they couldn't afford. Sent out to work as soon as he could earn, my father was unqualified and unskilled. He could not read or write on the day he met my mother and spent his early married life ducking and diving to survive.

Someone should write a thesis sometime on the effect of baldness on men. Some accept it with a shrug of the shoulders; others literally explode. My father couldn't handle it. Racked by insecurity, he tried to pretend it couldn't happen but soon the frustration and loathing began to burn like a fuse. Sooner or later, something had to give. Sooner and later we did: my sister gave, my mother gave, I gave. Together we survived the bombs until the war was ended and all that was left was the hurt.

Chapter Six
Ordinary Pictures

I'm not as normal as I appear.
> – Woody Allen

I don't mind that I'm fat. You still get the same money.
> – Marlon Brando

When I close my eyes and erase the darkness of my father's violence, the memories are normal. Brighter. I see a brother and sister, arguing in a bedroom; I hear the sound of Nat King Cole drifting over a garden wall; I feel the sun kissing my face on a summer holiday in Cornwall; I see two boys swapping football stickers at the back of the class in St Joseph's. I hear the hall door closing and Mum setting off for work. I see ordinary pictures of an ordinary life.

At the hub of this ordinary life was football, a love affair that began, as so many others have, with street games that started after school and finished after dark. The Wilsons, again, were more than generous, supplying the majority of our team in the shape of Philip, Kevin, Paul, Neil and Grant – their five splendid sons. My first organized games were played at St Philomena's Primary School and St Joseph's Secondary School, where we honed our skills and scuffed our shoes, playing with a tennis ball at lunchtime in the yard.

Tall and skinny, I was a good rather than gifted kid who played sometimes at centre forward but mostly at centre half. Outside school, I played with a club called Interfico, where one of the midfielders was a confident, long-haired, leather-

jacketed rocker called Andy Townsend. We didn't immediately hit it off. He lived ten miles away in Bexley Heath and
moved in a different clique, and it wasn't until he made his
début with Ireland that our friendship developed. Even as a kid,
it was obvious that Andy could play but it was equally obvious
that he didn't aspire to a career in the game. I worshipped the
idea but didn't believe I was good enough. The scouts never
seemed that interested in me.

After three years with 'Fico', I joined Kestrel Rangers at the
age of fourteen, mainly because they were another good team,
but mostly because I had discovered girls and was mad about
the sister of a guy who played there. I played well during my
first season with Kestrel and earned a selection to play for
North West Kent and was offered a trial at Charlton. The word
spread like wildfire around St Joseph's.

'Did you hear about Cascarino?'

'No.'

'He's going to sign for Charlton.'

A teacher pulled me aside and showered me with statistics
on the success/failure rate among wannabees and advised that
I proceed with caution. But he might as well have been talking
to the wall. I didn't want to know; I didn't heed a word. I
thought, 'Wow, this is it, the big time, a trial with Charlton
Athletic Football Club!' But when the moment arrived, and I
presented myself for the audition, the disillusion was crushing. 'Why have they asked so many other kids? Isn't this
supposed to be about me?' A year later, it was the same story
at Arsenal, when I was invited along to play in one of five
consecutive games. Over one hundred kids were called; a
handful were chosen. We were like peas on a conveyor belt.

Resigned to my fate, I had just about lost hope when Theo
Foley, whose son Adrian played for Kestrel, invited me to
spend some time with Queens Park Rangers. Theo was a
member of the coaching staff at Loftus Road. Each morning for
a week, we met at eight at Charlton station for the two-hour
journey by train and tube to the Rangers' training ground at

Greenford. It was tiring, but worth it. Stan Bowles and Phil Parkes were big names in England and it was great to be able to boast that you were sharing the same dressing room. I trained with the squad, played a couple of five-a-sides, and really thought I'd cracked it when I was invited to play for the reserves in a game at the end of the week. Nothing happened. I returned home and waited for the phone to ring but the offer never came. The message was clear. Professional football wasn't for me. I just wasn't good enough.

I continued to play for Kestrel Rangers until the end of the season and attended the annual awards presentation and dance. Incredibly, my friend's sister still hadn't succumbed to my charms but I was making headway in the midnight hour when I was distracted by a commotion in the hall. A group of local National Front thugs had gate-crashed the dance and were rounding on a team mate whose girlfriend was black. A punch was thrown and within seconds it was like a scene from the old cowboy films, with fists and boots flying everywhere and guys running at each other with chairs. The hall had emptied by the time the police arrived and the fighting had splintered and spread outside. Lending my support, I chased a group with some friends into an adjoining graveyard. It was pitch dark as we tracked them around the tombstones and finally cornered them. In the ensuing chaos, a hand grabbed and pulled me from behind; I turned instinctively and punched the bastard in the eye. It was a policeman! I hadn't noticed them arrive! Pinned immediately to the ground, I was taken to the station at Shooter's Hill and thrown into a cell. I'd never been locked up before and lost all track of time as night became morning and night again. After forty-odd hours, I was charged with assaulting a police officer and released. A date would be set for my appearance before the Crown.

While my brief sejourn behind bars was a sobering experience, it was nothing compared to my first experience of death. Of the five Wilson brothers, I was closest to Neil, the second youngest. Neil was two years older than me and though we had started to drift apart in our teenage years, there was a time, when growing up, we were pretty much inseparable. Molly Wilson was a huge Nat King Cole fan and you could always tell when Neil was home, because Nat would be stopped in mid-Mona Lisa and be replaced with something from Peter Frampton or Genesis. When he left school, Neil bought a motorbike and began studying to be a mechanic. One morning, while making his way to college, he was involved in a serious accident and was immediately rushed to hospital. I called to see him, about a week after the crash. He'd broken his leg, and looked, and sounded, as if he was in serious pain, but I never doubted for a moment that he would make a full recovery. It was the last time I saw him alive. His spleen burst shortly after my visit and he was rushed to emergency surgery, where he lapsed into a coma and died. I was never as upset in my life as I was at his funeral. Don Wilson was devastated, poor Molly was never the same; Neil was her little devil, her favourite. In the weeks and months that followed, Nat King Cole wasn't heard. I'd call to see her regularly and we'd sit and chat about Neil.

One night, shortly after he died, she asked me something that took me completely by surprise: 'Be honest with me, Tony, did he ever have sex?'

I didn't know; Neil had had a couple of girlfriends but it wasn't something we'd ever spoken about. My answer was instinctive.

'He did,' I replied. 'We laughed about it a couple of times.'

Her relief was palpable. 'Oh good,' she said. 'That's good.'

I left school with no regrets in the summer of '78. I also left without sitting my O levels and without a qualification. My mother wasn't happy but I was adamant I wasn't going back and I was soon earning a tidy £66 per week as a builder's labourer. It was tough, physical work and after three months of lugging bricks and mixing cement I spotted a vacancy in the local paper for what seemed a more interesting life. Don't ask me to explain my fascination with hair, but I decided to accept the position of apprentice hairdresser at a salon called J.B's in Bromley. There was one major drawback: as Saturday was the salon's busiest working day, I would have to give up playing football. I juggled the pros and cons and decided to turn the page.

There were eighteen other students in the hairdressing class at Erith College, where I was sent as part of my apprenticeship; all of them girls. Eighteen girls to myself!! I couldn't believe it! I thought: 'St Joseph's was never like this.' We trained on grey-haired old ladies who'd pay 20p to be butchered by our scissors or shampooed and set.

The salon's was a more interesting clientele. One afternoon, a middle-aged woman started feigning an orgasm as I washed her hair. Unsure how to react, I pretended at first not to hear.

'Oooh, harder,' she insisted, 'harder.'

So, rising to the challenge, I dug my fingers into her scalp and really got stuck in. She was frenetic; she just couldn't get enough.

'Ooooh . . . Yeah . . . Keep it up . . . Harder.'

She was a great character, an absolute nutter.

After a couple of months, I discovered that the one sure way to wet a girl's knickers was to sit her crookedly at the basin and allow the water to run down her back. It was embarrassing at times; the girl would stand up with what looked like a great big sweat mark on her back and I'd apologize profusely.

The late seventies was the era of the Clash, the Sex Pistols and punk, and though I was more a Mod by nature, I started going to a lot of punk concerts with a girl called Michelle Birch, who worked in the salon. We saw a lot of famous bands before they were famous and Michelle also introduced me to the strange but wonderful world of London's gay clubs. I was a bit reluctant at first but allowed her to drag me along to the Heaven in Charing Cross and we had a great night. That there were so many girls there was the biggest surprise, and so many straight men chatting them up. Boy George, with his high heels and outrageous sense of dress, most definitely wasn't straight and was just making a name for himself. But some of the others were characters too and fun to be around, and I was always fascinated by their conversations . . .

'Oh, look at that bitch.'

'Where?'

'Over there.'

'And look at him, showing his arse.'

'Yeah, he's trying to tease us.'

Later, when I was at Gillingham, I'd sneak back from time to time with Michelle for a night on the town but it wasn't something I could ever mention in the dressing room. It was bad enough that I had once been a hairdresser but if they ever found out I frequented gay clubs as well, my life would have been hell.

Although life at J.B's was almost always fun, after eighteen months I began to lose interest and realized that hairdressing wasn't for me. I missed playing football and the banter and wit of the dressing room and I wanted a job that would enable me to play. I started working for Nuttalls, the builders, where my father was a general foreman. Strangely, our relationship had slowly started to improve since our confrontation; it was as if, by drawing a line in the sand, I had at last earned his respect. But I also got a sense that the anger was wearing him down and that he was tired of the fighting. Relations improved further at Nuttalls when we began travelling to work together. Soon, we were almost communicating like a normal father and son. He knew I wanted to play again and mentioned it to a friend who knew the chairman of Crockenhill, an old village team that played in the Kent league. A week later, word came back that the manager, Steve Wishart, was prepared to take a look. 'Wish', who remains a great friend, often laughs that I turned up for my trial wearing a pair of black plimsolls and 'with your arse hanging out of your trousers'. But what I lacked in style, I made up for in enthusiasm; eighteen months of washing hair had left me with a fierce appetite to play.

ORDINARY PICTURES

In April 1981, two weeks after reporting for training, I made my début for Crockenhill as a centre half and held on to my place for the next game until twenty minutes from the end, when Paul Clark broke his leg and I was switched to centre forward. Short on options as the season wound to a close, Wish decided to leave me there for the derby against Erith and Belvedere. I drove to the game in my mother's car and had just gone over the bridge at Erith station when I was distracted by a good-looking girl on the pavement and smashed into the car in front. It wasn't the best omen to take to the game but I managed to score all three in our 3–1 win. My good form continued after the summer break when I began the new season with a goal against Herne Bay. Within a couple of months, word began to spread that Crockenhill had found a talent and I was invited for a trial in December by Keith Peacock, the Gillingham manager. Keith had watched me a couple of times but couldn't make up his mind. At the trial, I was told to watch from the side as he sent the first team out in a practice game against the reserves. Steve Bruce was the best player on the pitch and already showing the ability that would take him to Manchester United, but I tore into him the moment I went on, rugged and raw and mad to compete. 'It was like releasing a gorilla from a cage,' Keith laughed. But the gorilla had made his mark and was immediately offered a contract. The deal, one year at £100 per week was just £5 more than I was earning with Nuttalls, but the challenge was exciting and I decided to accept.

When the contract was drawn up (there was no transfer fee as such but as a gesture, Gillingham made a donation to Crockenhill of some tracksuits and equipment), I played one last game for Crockenhill. I can't quite remember now who it was against but do recall my horror the moment I entered the dressing room.

'The lads have decided you deserve a decent send off,' John Maloney announced. He dipped into a bag and placed a pink vibrator on the table. 'This is your present for after the game, ' he laughed. 'You are getting it, my son.'

FULL TIME

When the game started, I found it impossible to concentrate. At nineteen, I was a lot younger than the rest of them. I thought, 'Shit! They're not serious, are they? They're not really going to come at me with that thing?'

As soon as the game ended, I was grabbed by both ankles and upended in the showers. They split my legs, splashed soap on my bum and switched the plastic penis on. When I close my eyes, I can still hear the guffaws of Maloney and Johnny Hibbitt . . .

'Come on, you hairdresser poof!'

'You are getting it my son.'

'You're gonna love this, aren't you?'

But thankfully that's as far as it went.

Someone once said that we should treat our bodies like temples and care for them as if we are going to live for ever. That makes a lot of sense now as I creak towards middle age, but it wouldn't have meant much to me in 1982. Overnight, I went from a life of part-time football, junk food and late nights on the lash chasing totty with the lads to life of full-time football, junk food and late nights on the lash chasing totty with the lads. My attitude never changed; I continued to treat my body like a dustbin, and continued to get away with it.

I made my début as a professional on the first Tuesday of February, 1982, in a league game against Burnley at Turf Moor, after a speedy promotion to the first team that was, it's fair to say, more circumstance – a spate of injuries and suspensions – than design. I was quite nervous in the dressing room before going out but almost made a perfect start when I half-volleyed a knock down with my first touch which crashed off the Burnley cross bar. Although we were beaten 1–0, the game went well for me and I did enough to retain my place three days later in another away fixture at Chester, where I struggled to shake off a stomach bug and was substituted in the second half. Next up was the chance to make my home début against Wimbledon, but two blank sheets and a poor performance at

Chester had swayed the manager, who hinted that I wouldn't start and was unlikely to make the bench.

On the morning of the game, after a leisurely breakfast at home, I set out on my usual route by train from Orpington (via Sidcup) to Gillingham. It was 1.05 p.m. when I stepped on to the platform at Gillingham. Priestfield was a five-minute walk from the station. The instruction was to report to the ground at 1.45 p.m. Feeling slightly peckish, and with time on my hands, I decided to treat myself to a double Wimpey and chips and a Knickerbocker Glory. Indigestion started the moment I reached the dressing room and glanced at the team sheet on the noticeboard. There had to be some mistake! *'FUCK!'* I'd made the subs! I changed and tried to convince myself that the congealed mass of beef and cream and fried potatoes in my gut would soon work its way down but as I ran out for the warm up, my stomach was turning like an overloaded spin dryer. What was I going to do?

I considered waddling (running was out of the question) to the toilet and shoving my fingers down my throat but decided that twenty minutes to the kick-off, plus forty-five minutes to the end of the first half, plus fifteen minutes for half-time, equalled well over an hour before he'd consider making a change. There was still a chance I could pull it off. At five to three, I followed the team on to the pitch and took my place on the bench. After a bright, positive start, my fears were eased considerably when we quickly opened the scoring. But then, just fifteen minutes into the game, Dean White was badly injured and I was ordered to get stripped. My first appearance at Priestfield should have been a moment to cherish but all I could think about was the double Wimpey and chips; all I could see was the photograph next day in the papers: 'Stitched up! Tony Cascarino is stretchered off clutching his stomach, five minutes after coming on against Wimbledon.' Hyper-conscious of the need to pace myself, I eased into the game and survived until half-time. By the end, I was bombing around and even managed to score the final goal – my first as a professional

– in the 6–1 rout. It should have been a valuable lesson but nothing really changed; I dropped the Knickerbocker Glories but it was pretty much burgers as usual.

On the night before the next game, an away fixture at Exeter, I was sitting at home with my feet up when I was tempted to go for a drink with Chris 'Mac' McCarthy and some friends. I had resolved to rest and be professional, but Friday was always my favourite night of the week and I thought, 'I'll just nip out for a quick one and get back early.' One drink led to a disco bar in Dartford. At half past two, we had just finished dancing the night away when we were drawn into a fight with another group that quickly turned nasty and spilled outside. When the police arrived, I immediately took flight and was chased up the street by a copper. Aware of my pending appointment in court, and of the stink with Gillingham if I was caught, I sprinted clear, jumped a garden fence and hid. Mac was caught and taken to the station. 'Who's your mate?' he was asked. 'Allan bleedin' Wells!' When the coast was clear and the sirens had stopped wailing, I started walking home. St Paul's Cray is eleven miles from Dartford. I covered the first five on foot to Bexley mental home and decided to call a cab. The waiting time was forty-five minutes. I started walking and jogging again. At half past four, covered in sweat, I collapsed, exhausted, into bed.

I had only just shut my eyes, or so it seemed, when I was rudely awoken by a call from the club. I was late. The team were waiting. I had fifteen minutes to get to the Black Prince in Dartford or there'd be hell to pay. I leapt from the bed, reached frantically for a tracksuit and made the deadline with seconds to spare. I slept most of the way on the coach into London, and most of the journey to Exeter on the train. There were fifteen minutes to play when Keith Peacock ordered me on. The game finished 1–1. I didn't score . . .

In the four months between my début and the end of the season in May, I scored five league goals in twenty-four appearances (five as a sub) for Gillingham. I also made an appearance before the judges of the Crown Court, where the charges against me were dropped because the policeman couldn't properly identify his assailant – a fair ruling given how dark it was in the graveyard. Later that summer, after Portsmouth and Coventry made inquiries about buying me, Gillingham doubled my wages and hurried me to sign a new three-year deal. Within six months of joining, I'd become Gillingham's second-highest paid player (behind Bruce) and it had all come incredibly easy. A big fish in a small pool, I was living the life of Reilly. I was bulletproof.

Chapter Seven
Planes, Trains and Automobiles

People's backyards are much more interesting than their front gardens.

— John Betjeman

No other man-made device since the shields and lances of the ancient knights fulfils a man's ego like an automobile.

— Lord Rootes

After six months of life as a professional, it was aspects of the life I had never considered that surprised me most. Before signing for Gillingham I had never, for example, roomed with another man. I had played with other men and showered with other men and dined with other men and sipped with other men and fought with other men, but I'd never actually shared a room with another man. I had shared a room with women, and shared a bed with women, and enjoyed every moment of it, but the act of sharing with another man, of breathing the same air and peeing in the same bowl and washing in the same basin and talking on the same telephone and watching the same TV and sleeping under the same ceiling with another man, a complete stranger, sometimes in the bed alongside was an alien experience. And one that took a lot of getting used to.

Put yourselves in my shoes for a moment: you're nineteen years old, have just signed for Gillingham Football Club and are about to discover the strange new world of playing away from home. You drive to Carlisle or Lincoln or Huddersfield on the eve of the game and step from the coach into the lobby of the team hotel where the physio has pinned beside the lift a list with all the rooms. You examine the list and discover you've been paired with Q, a first team regular you've trained with, but hardly spoken to before. Dinner is served in a function room downstairs. You sit listening to the banter around the table, then retire to the room to watch whatever Q fancies on TV before drifting off to sleep . . . Before Q drifts off, that is. You, unfortunately, have always been a light sleeper and with every sense heightened, just the gentle whisper of his breathing is enough to keep you awake. And then he farts and begins to snore and you know the night will be long. You toss and turn into the early hours until the frustration finally exhausts you. When morning comes and you open your eyes, Q is staring at the ceiling with his finger up his nose and a Wigwam in his bed.

'Morning Tone, sleep well?' he enquires, completely unabashed.

'Yeah, great thanks, Q,' you lie.

He casts off the sheets and walks bollock naked to the bathroom, defiantly parading his veiny sausage to the tune of Abba's 'Voulez-vous'. You shake your head in disbelief: 'This is the pits!' You've never seen an aroused penis before, except, obviously, your own. After a long and laborious pee that considerably lowers his mast, Q exits the bathroom, yawning and scratching his nuts, and makes for the bowl of fruit on the bedside table, unaware and unconcerned that two pubic hairs have dropped into the grapes.

'Would you like some fruit?' he offers, extending the bowl.

'No thanks,' you decline.

Why, you wonder, didn't they warn you about this in *Shoot*?

The real problem with sharing a room is that you never know who you are going to be lumbered with. As in the film *Planes, Trains and Automobiles*, there's always another nutcase waiting around the corner but after eighteen years of smelly bastards, tight gits, sleepers, alcoholics, comedians, insomniacs, depressives, faithful husbands and serial adulterers, I can safely say I've had, and mostly enjoyed, them all. Rooming with Andy Townsend and Niall Quinn always reminded me of married life . . .

'You put the tea on, love, I'll get the biscuits.'

'You sleep in that bed, love, I'll sleep in this one.'

Throw your bag in the wrong place or leave a razor blade in the bath and you were always sure of a bollocking. Andy controlled the TV remote for the best part of ten years! Niall used to nag me more than my wife. Bernie Slaven, another great character from my Ireland years, used to call his dog every night. I'd be sitting in the bed alongside and Bernie would be howling like Lassie into the phone 'Woof, woof, aru, aru, woof!' He'd be kissing the receiver and lavishing affection – 'Hello, lovey dovey' – on a dog! The first time it happened, I nearly wet myself and told him he was completely mad. Bernie, being Bernie, just laughed.

Sometimes, things were a bit more complicated. There was one former team mate who was caught and outed by the tabloids for having an affair and whenever his wife phoned and he wasn't around, it was an absolute disaster . . .

'Hello, Tony, it's Y.'

'Hello, Y. How are you, love?'

'Fine thanks. Where's X?'

'He's not in the room at the moment, he's, er, down having dinner.'

Pause. She's thinking: 'He's off shagging someone.' I'm thinking: 'Oh, for fuck's sake, she thinks he's off shagging someone.'

'Is he having dinner? Is he really having dinner?'

'Course he is, Y. I've just come up myself.'

'It's very late . . .'

'Tell you what, as soon as he gets back, I'll get him to give you a call.'

'What do you mean, as soon as he gets back? Back from where?'

'Back to the room . . . back from his dinner.'

'Oh, right, fine. Thanks Tony.'

Ten minutes later, X returns; he's been playing cards in another room.

'Your missus has been on. She's fretting. You'd better give her a call.'

'Oh fuck.'

He dives on to the phone and a heated argument ensues. Exasperated, X hands me the receiver, the veins popping in his neck: *'Tell her where I've been!'*

The problem, unfortunately, was often compounded on the occasions when X wasn't playing cards. There was always great teamwork when a player had a woman to bed. X, for example, would switch with Z, who had a room to himself, and Z would move in for the night with me. Inevitably, the phone would ring. *'Don't answer it!'* I'd scream. 'It might be X's wife! She'll want to know where he is and why you're in the room.' There was rarely a dull moment.

The other peculiarity of my new career was the unique brand of humour that existed in the dressing room. During my time on the building sites, I'd worked with some right hard cases and always been amused by the humour in the canteen. The dressing room, however, was a much darker place. Around the time of my professional début, a team mate, whose wife was expecting a baby girl, didn't show for training one morning.

'What's happened to X?' I asked. 'How come he's not in?'

'Oh, his missus has lost her baby,' someone said.

'Shit,' I said, 'that's terrible.'

'Yeah,' he said, 'I heard she was drop-dead gorgeous.'

At first I thought I was hearing things but it would soon become routine. Chelsea was the worst. At Chelsea, it was open season, seven days a week. There were times when I'd think: 'My God! I can't believe you've said that!' And after a while, I was just as bad as anyone else. I'm not sure what it is about football but there seems to be much more respect in other professions, a limit to how far you can go for a laugh. In football, there are no limits. In football, in English football, a black humour pervades that at times borders on the depraved.

The bulletproof coating I'd worn since my début against Burnley first began to chip nine months later in November '82, when we were drawn to play Tottenham in a League (Milk) Cup at Priestfield. It was a huge game for Gillingham and because of my form since the start of the season I was presented as the rising star who would send the prima donnas packing. Spurs sent most of their best players – Steve Archibald, Graham Roberts, Glenn Hoddle, Ray Clemence and Garth Crooks – and I was aware, walking out, that it was my first real test, but I completely froze after missing an early chance. When Spurs went 3–1 up at the start of the second half, Roberts couldn't resist turning the screw. 'What! *You*'re the secret weapon! *You*'re going to knock us out of the Cup! You must be joking! You haven't kicked the fucking thing yet.' It should have been enough to get me going but instead I withdrew even further into my shell. Nothing was said in the dressing room afterwards but I was more than aware I'd bottled it and endured a long and sleepless night. Was I really good enough to play at the top? If Spurs were the barometer and I hadn't had a kick, maybe I was just fooling myself? For the first time in my career I began to doubt. And then, fourteen months later, the doubt found a voice . . . .

On the last Tuesday of January 1984, Priestfield was packed to capacity for the visit of Everton in the FA Cup. Three days earlier, we had returned from Goodison Park as heroes after holding the first-division side to a 0–0 draw and the ground buzzed with hope that we could somehow win the replay. After ninety minutes there was stalemate, which continued until the final moments of extra time, when Everton pushed everyone forward in one last desperate attempt to secure a winning goal. I was standing on the halfway line, completely unmarked, when the ball was suddenly hoofed to me from the siege of our defence. I turned, looked up and started running toward the Everton goal. I looked up again. I couldn't believe my eyes! I was on my own! *There wasn't an Everton player within thirty fucking yards!* All I had to do to knock Everton out of the Cup was beat their goalkeeper, Neville Southall.

I'm not sure how many strides I had taken when I first heard the voice. Or at what stage the crowd stopped shouting and were quiet. Suddenly, those five seconds alone felt like hours. It was as if I was running in slow motion and suspended in time, oblivious to everything except the giant shadow of Neville Southall and this strange, irritating, voice . . .

'*Shuuush.*'

'I'm sorry?'

'*Quiet! We're holding our breath.*'

'Who are you?'

'*I'm the eight-year-old boy in row twelve. I'm Bill from Bromley and Steve from Sidcup, who haven't missed a game for fifteen years. I'm Keith Peacock and Steve Bruce and Old Buster Collins the sponge man. I'm the voice of every Gillingham supporter in the ground, desperately hoping you'll take this chance but worried you'll fuck up.*'

'Thanks for the vote of confidence.'

'*Don't mention it. Just take your time and think about it for a moment.*'

'I'm thinking.'

'*You're thirty yards clear.*'

'I'm aware of that.'

'*There's only the keeper to beat.*'

'That too.'

'*Any striker worth his salt will put this ball in the net.*'

'Yeah, but . . .'

'*This is your big chance.*'

'It's not as easy as it looks, you know.'

'*You're shitting yourself, aren't you?*'

'No, I . . .'

'*You're going to miss.*'

'CLEAR OFF!'

'You're going to make a bollocks of it.'

Southall started to feint and fidget . . . I was almost close enough but couldn't figure him out . . . Panic was clouding my brain like a fog . . . He narrowed the angle and stood his ground . . . Impulsively I reached for the trigger and kicked an awful shot that almost dribbled into his hands.

'You clumsy fucking twat.'

'Sorry, I . . .'

'You gave him the ball!'

'I know but . . .'

'You literally presented it to him.'

'Yeah, did you hear the gasp in the crowd? I want to bury myself.'

'Congratulations.'

'For what?'

'I've seen some misses in my time but that was different class.'

'Thanks.'

'But look on the bright side – you're a household name.'

'How's that?'

'They'll be showing repeats of it for years.'

On those rare occasions when I've bumped into the Everton manager, Howard Kendall, since, he smiles and reminds me of the night I saved his job. I probably did. Everton won the second replay 3–0 and advanced to the next round. I returned to scoring goals against the Lincolns and Exeters, with a scar from the miss that took a long, long time to heal. They showed repeats of it for years . . .

In the summer of 1985, at the end of my fourth season at Gillingham, I paid £39,500 for a new house in Bexley. Still living with my parents, for four years I had dithered about buying a place of my own but was unable to take the decision. My father was the dilemma. Although he had never apologized or addressed what had happened in the past, our relationship had turned full circle. From the tentative beginning of shared journeys to work, he'd become a Gillingham supporter and by 1985 was almost the father I'd always wished I'd had. Ironically, the closer we became, the harder it was for me to leave home. I knew what would happen. My mother had spelt it out . . .

If the night of the broken glass had proved a watershed in our relationship, it also triggered a change in his relationship with Mum. In the years that followed, as his anger began to recede, a much rounder and more likeable person began to emerge. Suddenly, he was cooking dinners and tidying the house. Suddenly, he was coming to games and cheering me on. Suddenly, he was treating my mother with kindness and respect. Suddenly, he was a man transformed. Hugely impressed with his ability to change, I embraced the new Dominic and welcomed him home. My mother couldn't. My mother didn't want to know.

That same summer, a few weeks before I eventually moved out, she arrived home from work one evening to find him barbecuing in the garden. 'What do you think you're doing,' she fumed. 'Look at all the smoke going over the [neighbour's] wall!' It was a ridiculous argument, the latest in a long and deliberate campaign to undermine him at every chance. Undermining him, you see, meant an argument. And an argument meant he was mad. And when he was mad, it reminded her of the way he used to be. And when she was reminded about the way he used to be, it made her feel better about what she had sworn to do. My mother had suffered too much to forgive and forget. One night, perhaps during the storm when he was smashing up her kitchen, perhaps when he was kicking and punching her son, she made a promise to herself. On the day Mandy was married, she shared it with me: 'The day you leave, Tony, I leave.' And so it was . . .

A week after I'd moved to Bexley, my mother walked out. That night, when my father called to see me, he was absolutely distraught. I made some tea and we sat and chatted in the kitchen. It was probably the first real conversation we'd ever had. When he told me he had never been unfaithful, I believed him. He was never a womanizer, never a drinker, but he'd screwed up big time and the penny had finally dropped. I sat and sympathized as best I could and invited him to stay for a while. He stayed for a year. That night, as I twisted and turned in bed, I couldn't help thinking what a strange irony it was that the man who had made me cry for so long should end up crying on my shoulder. And what an unexpected twist that we should start living together because the woman who had protected me from him for so long, was gone.

The other significant development of 1985 was the arrival of a new goalkeeper on loan from Notts County called Seamus McDonagh, who also happened to be the Republic of Ireland number one. One afternoon, after I'd quizzed him about life as an international and informed him of my roots, Seamus promised to pass my name to the Irish manager, Eoin Hand. A few weeks later, I was invited to play for an Irish selection in a testimonial game for Jimmy Holmes in Dublin.

It was my first ever visit to Ireland. The game was played on a lovely sunny evening in Dalymount Park and I scored and played well enough against a Glenn Hoddle selection to grab the headlines next day in the *Irish Independent*: 'Weather and fans turn up as Hand finds striker.' A month later, I was named in the squad for a World Cup qualifying game in Switzerland. My international career was about to begin.

There are two memories of the afternoon we arrived in Berne. The first was the magnificent view of the lake from our hotel and the breathtaking splendour of the Swiss countryside. I remember looking out of my bedroom window and thinking, 'God, what a place! Ibiza was never like this.' The second was being introduced to the great Liam Brady, who had travelled separately from his home in Milan. Of the many stars on the team at that time – Frank Stapleton, Mark Lawrenson, Jim Beglin, Gerry Daly, Paul McGrath, Dave O'Leary – none shone brighter than Liam Brady. As a boy, I'd made many a trip with Mac to Highbury just to watch him play, and it was a genuine thrill to meet him in the flesh. After dinner, he invited me to join the card school, where I was promptly relieved of my match fee. He was a smooth operator, on and off the field; I can still see him now with his fashionable Italian shades, chewing on a sweet and studying his hand like the Sundance Kid.

If Liam was the undisputed star of the group, the team captain, Frank Stapleton, wasn't far behind, still scoring goals for Manchester United and one of the biggest names in the game. When I learned that we had been paired to room together, I couldn't wait to tell my mates. I was also extremely nervous and self-conscious, and couldn't make up my mind whether to engage in conversation or to give him some space.

Anyone who has ever played with Frank and is honest will tell you he has never been the easiest bloke in the world to get on with. He's an extremely dour man who takes himself awfully seriously. There used to be a running joke in the game that when Frank woke up each morning, he'd race to the bathroom and smile, just to get it over with. All this meant nothing to me in 1985. Star gossip rarely filtered as low as the third division. We are talking pauper and prince here; bright-eyed owner of second-hand Ford Capri meets BMW-driving superstar he has always regarded with awe.

An hour passed and although niceties had been exchanged we still hadn't really broken the ice. I'd had a couple of signals from Frank that he wasn't overly enamoured with the idea of sharing with me but I was determined to give it my best shot. Then I noticed he was reading a new BMW catalogue. Cars are a second language in the game and it seemed an ideal opportunity to establish cordial relations, so I cleared my throat and decided to go for it. His response would colour my impression of him for life.

'Are you thinking of buying a new BMW, Frank?'

He lowered the catalogue and looked across. 'Naah,' he smirked. 'Can't afford it.'

There was no mistaking the put-down. I wanted to jump off the bed and chin him.

Mick McCarthy was also on that team. Mick didn't have Brady's class and wasn't a superstar like Stapleton, but there was a steel about him I didn't always appreciate although I often admired it. Three months earlier, he'd played against the Swiss in Dublin and as we left the hotel for the game, he warned me about their big centre half.

'Watch Egli,' he said. 'He hits off the ball, dirty bastard. We had a right old battle in Dublin.'

'He can't do that,' I gulped. 'He'll get sent off.'

'Naah, crafty bugguh has it down to a fine art. Don't let him push you around.'

We arrived at the stadium and sure enough, during the warm-up, I noticed this huge, hairy bear of a man staring at me. He reminded me of Brutus from *Popeye*. Mick noticed him too and ran across.

'That's 'im!' he thundered, pointing his finger. 'That's the fucker there!'

'Thanks a lot, Mick,' I said, wishing he'd been more discreet.

Egli continued his mind games through the warm-up. I poked out my tongue at him and made a silly face. He didn't even blink. 'Oh dear,' I thought, jogging back to the dressing room. 'Maybe that wasn't such a good idea.' When the game started, he clouted me at the first opportunity but I immediately walloped him back to let him know I wasn't having it. I'm not sure what Eoin Hand made of it, but Mick was definitely impressed.

The game went badly for us. Frank missed a chance just before the end but overall, 0–0 was probably a fair result. Foolishly, I'd started with a brand-new pair of boots and my feet were badly blistered. Although I hadn't scored, I'd given a good account of myself and as I limped towards the dressing room, a small group of supporters began chanting my name, using flat Dublin accents that sounded odd and almost comical at first.

'Toe-knee-cass-carino.'
'Toe-knee-cass-carino.'
It was nice. I liked it. I would love it later.

Despite my promising début, the draw had seriously compromised the Republic's chances of qualifying from the group and the pressure was really on when we travelled to Moscow to play the Soviet Union a month later. Although gifted with many brilliant individuals, the team clearly weren't playing to their potential and the knives were out for the manager, who was savaged by the press in the build-up. Although I hadn't been around for long enough to form an opinion, I liked Eoin and found him extremely personable, but one aspect of his management style struck me as odd. At a meeting on the night before the game in Moscow, he invited comments from three of the team's most experienced players: Brady, Lawrenson and Stapleton. Liam and Mark both declined to speak but when Frank stood up he delivered what was essentially a directive on how we were to play!

My second international, like many of my 'second' games for teams over the years, proved a huge disappointment. Liam was very encouraging in the dressing room before we ran out. 'If you come short to me,' he said, 'they will be right up close. I want you to come, then spin and go, and I'll put it over the centre-half's head.' And invariably he did, but I played poorly and was substituted after an hour in the 2–0 defeat.

The final game in the group was a home tie against Denmark a month later. With qualification now beyond us, there wasn't a great deal of enthusiasm for the game, or the team, amongst the Irish public. Mick Byrne, ever the optimist, predicted a crowd of 25,000 at Lansdowne Road. 'There wouldn't be 25,000 if the Beatles were playing today,' he was told. On the day, a mere 15,000 streamed through the turnstiles. I played pretty well and laid on a goal for Frank, but the Danes ripped us apart in a 4–1 hiding that was easily the heaviest defeat I've experienced in Dublin. As expected, Eoin duly resigned as manager and was replaced the following spring by Jack

FULL TIME

Charlton. Having enjoyed my first taste of international football, I hoped my visits to Dublin would continue, but it was soon obvious to me that the new manager wasn't a fan. 'I went to watch you once and thought you were a fat, lazy bastard!' Jack later explained. Two years would pass before he changed his mind.

Chapter Eight
Room with a View

The Man (Edward G. Robinson): 'Gets down to what it's all about, doesn't it? Making the wrong move at the right time.'
The Kid (Steve McQueen): 'Is that what it's all about?'
The Man: 'Like life, I guess. You're good, kid, but as long as I'm around you're second best. You might as well learn to live with it.'

– The Cincinnati Kid

By the summer of 1987, I had played 263 games, scored 110 goals and spent six seasons with Gillingham in the third division, which seems a long time in hindsight but certainly didn't feel that way at the time. The club was a big happy family and I was the favourite son; popular with the fans, I was always in the papers or on local TV and revelled in the role of smalltown hero. My experiences with Ireland, however, had broadened my horizons. When you've played in front of a capacity crowd at the Lenin Stadium, shared a dressing room with Liam Brady and flicked through the pages of a BMW catalogue, you suddenly begin to yearn for bigger and brighter things. And by the summer of '87, it was time to move on.

My final season at Priestfield was easily my most successful. In May, I was voted Player of the Year after scoring five of the goals that beat Sunderland in an epic two-leg play-off. The win earned us another do-or-die game with Swindon, where the prize was promotion to the second division for the first time in Gillingham's history. Had we achieved it, there was every chance I would have renewed my contract and stayed for another season, but we were edged out over three games, and after a short holiday in Marbella, I returned to London and signed for Millwall.

That the only other option was a move to Ipswich was surprising, given my performances that season. Maybe it was because *It Will Be All Right On The Night* was still showing reruns of my gift to Neville Southall, that the big clubs had all taken a look and kept their chequebooks in their pockets. I remember a chief scout at Chelsea explaining to me once that he had watched me at Gillingham. 'I just couldn't make up my mind about you. You were either very good or not very good – I just couldn't decide.' Inconsistency was the bane of my career until I moved to France. There was no such thing as an average performance with me; I was either brilliant or crap – there was no middle ground. One week it was: 'Fuckin 'ell! Did you see Cascarino last night? He tore the arse out of them!' And the next it was: 'Who's that big lazy fucker up front? He never moved!' The reason, of course, for these erratic swings in form was my appalling diet and the fact that I didn't look after myself. Like an old dog that only responds to his master's boot, I needed to be whipped around the training ground and playing regularly to perform at my best. And when I did, I was close to unstoppable.

John Docherty, a 48-year-old Glaswegian, was the first manager I ever had who recognized this. On my first day at Millwall, he invited me into his office at the Den and offered me some cake and a glass of Coke.

'Do you take a drink?' he inquired.

'Yeah, from time to time,' I said.

'You do know you have to be fit to drink?'

'How do you mean, John?'

'What I mean is that if you continue drinking and you're not a good athlete, you won't be playing for me.'

'Oh . . . yeah . . . right.'

And then he said: 'Now enjoy the cake, because it's the last you'll be having while I'm in charge. I'm going to whip your arse into shape.' And when pre-season training began, he was as good as his word.

Millwall invested hugely that summer in the push for promotion to Division One. After forking out £225,000 for me, they signed George Lawrence from Southampton for £160,000, Kevin O'Callaghan from Portsmouth for £85,000 and Steve Wood from Reading for £80,000. That I was easily the biggest signing cut no ice with Teddy Sheringham, who had struck me as a right cold fish in training and who started ordering me around in our opening game of the season at Middlesborough.

Teddy was four years younger than me and had been at the club for years, but for ninety minutes it was as if I was his understudy.

'Go there!'

'Do this!'

'Chase back!'

'Hold on!'

I thought, 'Wait a fucking minute! I'm the 25-year-old! I'm the one they've paid all the money for! This never happened at Gillingham!' But I soon learned that this was Teddy's way. He had to be boss.

Our second game together was on a hot and humid August afternoon at the Den against Barnsley, when I headed home a Terry Hurlock cross, six minutes after the interval, to score my first goal for my new club. Five minutes later, Teddy seized upon a parried clearance from the box to put us 2–0 in front. When we ended the game with a notch each on our belts, the first blows in our personal, season-long battle for supremacy had been struck. And then the cheers turned to jeers when we didn't score again for a month.

Millwall was the hardest club in the country when you weren't playing well and its supporters could be absolutely vicious but again, it was Teddy who showed the way. I remember once during the drought, following him down the tunnel when a 'fan' suggested he wasn't trying hard enough. Or to use his exact words: 'Oi! Sheringham! Get that fucking piano off your back!' Teddy carried on as if nothing had happened. He didn't even blink. I tried to present the same impregnable sheen when the venom was directed at me but because mine was fake, the bastards always got to me. Teddy genuinely never let it bother him. He could play, and he knew he could play, and no loudmouth on the terraces was ever going to convince him otherwise. Teddy is the only player I know who could miss three one-on-ones and still try to chip the goalkeeper! The crowd could be absolutely baying for his blood but he would just carry on. He had more self-belief and confidence than any player I'd ever known. And after a while his confidence began to rub off on me . . .

The drought lasted until the end of September when we both scored in the 2–0 defeat of West Bromwich Albion. A month later the goal tally was 6–4 in his favour. November belonged to me (7–1); December was his (5–3); and it was tit for tat until the last game of the season. The rivalry was bad news for the rest of the division. Teams were unable to cope with our lethal blend of power and skill and hated playing against us. With every game, the bond between us grew. Teddy is a policeman's son and it shows occasionally in his mannerisms. Sometimes, you'll bounce something off him, expecting an immediate response and he'll just look at you, blank.

'Ted? Ted? Please say something Ted.'

He isn't a joker and can seem a bit distant when you meet him first but he likes a good time. I have always admired him as a player and a friend.

If the more rigorous training regime and the confidence gleaned from Teddy were the two critical factors in my successful début for Millwall, the third was undoubtedly my life-long addiction to a very different game. From the moment I watched my grandfather upend the kitchen table, I have always been fascinated by cards. I could play a three-card break before I could read or write. Stud? American? Five card? Omaha? Draw? For Tony Cascarino read the Cincinnati Kid.

Although I had always played for money, it wasn't until I became a professional footballer that the stakes were raised.

It started when a team mate at Gillingham introduced me to a car dealer called Lucky Jim and I was invited to join a card school that convened in a social club in Sparrows Lane, which was just across the road from the Charlton training ground. Every day from Monday to Friday, I'd stash a grand in my tracksuit pocket after training and drive to Sparrows Lane. The games started at two and went on for as long as there was money on the table, sometimes finishing at seven, sometimes finishing at midnight or into the early hours. For three years, I kept a record of my winnings and averaged an annual profit of £15,000. There were losings too – I lost my car once, a Ford Sierra – but I was generally pretty good when it came to knowing when to quit.

Poker, you quickly learn, is a game of consummate skill. For sure, there's an element of luck involved but the higher the stakes, the more craft it takes to win. I knew I could play a bit but also knew there was a difference between playing for pleasure and playing for real. I played for pleasure. The pros played for real. It was only when you observed them in the casinos that you truly appreciated what the difference was. Teddy thought I was crazy. He'd come along and watch from time to time but never got involved. I loved playing with the card school – I loved it more than playing football. It was under my skin, part of me. I had it bad – so bad, there were days when I couldn't wait to leave the training ground. And because I was passing on snacks and dinners, the games kept my weight in check.

The group that played at Sparrows Lane were a motley crew of car dealers and duckers and divers. Sometimes, because of the sums of money involved, we would switch venues for security and play at other clubs. The Butterfly Club in Eltham was one of our least frequented locations as it was awkward to find and situated in a lane which wasn't that accessible. One afternoon, a few months after I'd joined Millwall, we were about an hour into a game when there was a knock on the door.

'Who is it?'

There was no reply.

'What do you want?'

Again there was no response. I was nearest the door, but like the rest, was too engrossed to leave the table. There was another knock.

'It's open!' I roared.

And with that, the door slammed back and four armed and masked raiders burst into the hall. I nearly shit myself. I jumped out of the seat and dropped everything on to the floor. They pulled the telephone wires, checked to see if anyone was in the toilet and ordered us to empty our pockets into a hold-all. As they were leaving, one of the lads had a gun shoved into his face. 'I know who you are, and you know who I am, so there'd better not be any problems,' he was warned. There wasn't. We sat in silence, too stunned and afraid to move.

There was no great rush to involve the police. We would take our medicine and next time be more careful. In the days that followed, the overriding emotion when the group reconvened was one of relief that Nutnut hadn't been present. Nutnut, as his name suggests, wasn't exactly the most balanced member of the group and used to arrive some days with up to £20,000 in a plastic bag. Nutnut, we agreed, would have regarded any confrontation between himself and four armed raiders as an even call. They'd have had to kill him to take his money. And he would not have gone down alone.

On the first Wednesday of April, we arrived at Elland Road for one of our biggest tests of the season. The previous Saturday, a crowd of almost 14,000 – the biggest at the Den for ten years – had witnessed our 2–1 win over the division leaders Aston Villa. We were now fourth in the table, with six games to play, and trailed Villa by three points and Middlesborough and Blackburn by a point. For Millwall, the only London club never to play in Division One, the game against Leeds would be a critical test in the drive for promotion. But for me, there was another motivation.

As I ran out to warm up, I noticed Jack Charlton chatting with Kevin O'Callaghan in a corridor outside the dressing room. More than two years had passed since my last game for the Republic of Ireland. In sixteen games during his time at the helm, Jack had watched me once at Gillingham but never included me in a squad. For months I'd been dropping hints in interviews about how desperate I was to resume my international career. But the team had just qualified for the European Championship finals, so it wasn't as if my country needed me. And Jack wasn't the type who was easily coerced. When our paths finally crossed in the corridor at Elland Road, he glanced across and acknowledged me with a nod but said nothing. Had he come to visit some of his old pals, I wondered, or made the trip especially for me? It didn't matter. He was there. This was my chance.

When the game started, I ripped into the Leeds back-four like a man possessed and scored after seven minutes, latching on to a long clearance from Brian Horne, to drive the ball past the Leeds keeper Mervyn Day. Determined to continue after the perfect start, I was twice denied by two brilliant saves from Day before setting up the winning goal for Terry Hurlock, five minutes into the second half. When it was over, I noticed Jack briefly in the players' lounge and hoped for a sign that I'd impressed, but he was locked into a conversation with Peter Lorimer. Two days later, however, when he was quoted in the *Sun* as saying it was 'the best I've ever seen Tony play', I was sure I'd done enough. The Republic were due to play Yugoslavia in the first of a series of warm-up games for the European Championships, three weeks later in Dublin. I hoped, and waited, but Jack never called . . .

Meanwhile, at Millwall, the push for promotion had reached fever pitch when we moved four points clear after successive wins over Plymouth and Bournemouth. As the campaign entered its final week, we had just started preparing the next game with Stoke when Jack contacted the club and asked that I be released to fly to Dublin, following the late withdrawals of John Aldridge (hamstring) and Niall Quinn (chicken pox) from his squad. Reg Burr, the Millwall chairman, wouldn't entertain it. 'Only a little while ago, Charlton was saying Cascarino was no good for the Irish team because he lacked pace. So he's changed his mind,' he told the *Daily Mail*. 'We have three hard games in a week to make history and we just cannot afford to release Tony right now. I think he understands why.' And I did. But I'd have preferred it if it hadn't been trumpeted so loudly in print. When you were as far down the pecking order as I was with Ireland – sixth behind Aldridge, Stapleton, Quinn, John Byrne and Dave Kelly – the last thing you needed was to incur Jack Charlton's wrath.

Two days after our 2–0 defeat of Stoke, Millwall clinched promotion, and the championship, with a 1–0 win at Hull. For the first time in 103 years the club would play in Division One. Four days later, amid scenes of jubilant celebration at the Den, we played our last game of the season against Blackburn, when the only outstanding issue was the ongoing battle with Teddy, which was tied at twenty-three goals each. Duped by the carnival atmosphere in the ground, I left my game in Hull as Blackburn brushed us aside to win 4–1. Millwall's last goal of the season was scored by the same player who had scored their first. That was the thing about Teddy: he always wanted it more.

Two weeks of mostly rest and relaxation later, the call I'd been waiting for finally arrived and I was drafted into the squad for a friendly between Ireland and Poland in Dublin. My first contact with Jack was a brief handshake in the lobby of the team hotel but it wasn't until we started preparing for the game that I caught my first real glimpse of the man in charge. We were practising set pieces and had moved from corners to free kicks. Jack was explaining to Ronnie Whelan exactly what he wanted done; I was facing away from him with Kevin Sheedy in the wall. It was hot. The session grew tedious. Bored with our role as mere bricks in the wall, Sheedy and I had just started to shadow box when I was suddenly aware of a hush and Jack's presence on my shoulder. He was *not* amused.

'What do you think you're doing, you stupid fucking bastard?' he fumed.

'Sorry, Jack,' I choked, 'we were just having a bit of a laugh.'

'A bit of a laugh! A bit of a fucking laugh!! We're trying to get some serious work done here and I look around and you're shadow boxing with fucking Sheedy!'

'Sorry, Jack, I just . . .'

'Just my arse! Pay attention, you stupid pair of bastards!'

Sure any chance I'd had of ever playing again for Ireland had disappeared, I was surprised at his good humour later, over dinner. 'And what were you up to today, Cascarino, you silly buggah?' he chuckled. And even more surprised when he named me in the team. It was nice to know he didn't bear grudges.

In hindsight, because it certainly didn't occur to me at the time, my performance during those first thirty-two minutes against Poland was probably the most important of my career. First impressions were important with Jack; had I ignored his instructions or played badly and been substituted, there was a fair chance I wouldn't have worn a green shirt again. But when I scored in the thirty-second minute, following up a Ronnie Whelan free that was fumbled by the Polish keeper, the manager was happy. And when Jack was happy, your future with his team was secure.

That night, after returning to the team hotel for a meal, I headed back into the city with a group of the lads to a nightclub called Rumours, a favourite haunt of the team at the time. Footballers are seldom happier than when together out on the town and having just scored my first international goal, I was happier than most as I supped and danced into the early hours. I'm not sure what time it was when I stumbled out of the door to join the small queue for taxis. Or where my team mates had gone. I knew it was late. And that I'd had too much to drink. And that I would definitely have returned to the team hotel, if what happened hadn't happened as I was getting into the taxi.

But what do you say to a good-looking girl, who follows you from a nightclub and hitches a lift in your taxi when it's late and you've had a few drinks and you're still on a high from the goal you scored against Poland? What do you say when she smiles and gives you a squeeze and says, 'Your place or mine?', leaving you in absolutely no doubt that she wants your seed. What do you say when it's a week before Jack selects the squad for the European Championships and you've just got back in the frame and are desperate to make a favourable impression? Let me tell you what I said. I said: 'Fuck the team hotel.' I said: 'Fuck the team.' I said: 'Let's go to your place – mine's a little crowded.' I said: 'Honey, what's your name?'

The taxi took us south, to a house somewhere in the suburbs. We went inside, and ripped into each other like crazed animals, then dropped like crazed animals who've been shot with tranquillizing darts. When I opened my eyes again it was six thirty in the morning. I thought: 'Fuck! Where am I?' I thought: 'Fuck! How did I get here?' I thought: 'Fuck! Gotta get back to the team hotel as quick as possible!' I thought: 'Fuck! Who's she?'

I gathered my crumpled clothes from the trail on the floor and splashed some water on my face in the bathroom, where the view from the window was of a garden which backed on to a graveyard. I thought: 'If Sarah finds out about this, that's where they'll bury me.' Sarah was my fiancée. We were due to be married six weeks later.

Chapter Nine
Kiss of the Scorpion

I'm tired of all this nonsense about beauty being only skin deep. That's deep enough. What do you want – an adorable pancreas?

    – Jean Kerr, *The Snake has All the Lines*

If somebody says 'I love you' to me, I feel as though I have a pistol pointed at my head. What can anybody reply under such conditions but that which the pistol holder requires? 'I love you, too'.

    – Kurt Vonnegut, *Wamperers, Foma and Granfallons*

A scene from the movies that has always struck a chord with me is one of the opening scenes from *The Crying Game* where Jody (Forest Whittaker) tells Fergus (Stephen Rea) the story of the scorpion and the frog. It goes as follows. A scorpion wants to cross a river but he can't swim, so he goes to a frog, who can, and asks for a ride. The frog says, 'If I give you a ride on my back you'll go and sting me!' The scorpion replies, 'It would not be in my interest to sting you, since as I'll be on your back we both will drown.' The frog thinks about this logic for a while and accepts the deal, takes the scorpion on his back and braves the waters. Halfway over he feels a burning spear in his side and realizes the scorpion has done him after all. As they both sink beneath the waves, the frog cries out, 'Why did you sting me, Mr Scorpion? For now we both will drown.' The scorpion replies, 'I can't help it. It's in my nature.'

While I have always believed, deep down, that I'm

essentially a decent human being, there have been times, I must admit, when I've done things I'm not particularly proud of. Joanne springs to mind. We met, when we were seventeen, at a club called the Link near her home in Orpington and went out together for the best part of five years. Jo invested hugely in the relationship and was always a rock of support as my career shifted from the hairdressing salon to the building site to the football field. Kind, decent and affectionate, Jo believed she had found her Mr Right, a man who would provide the love and stability she'd never had as a child. But, as Jody reminds us in *The Crying Game*, there are two kinds of people in life: givers and takers, scorpions and frogs. And in the summer of '84, just when she thought she had a giver on board, just when she wanted him to make a commitment, Joanne was stung.

I should have explained that I didn't want to settle down, that I was too immature to sign a contract with one person for the rest of my life. Honesty was the least she deserved after five years of love and companionship. But a scorpion does what's in its nature when confronted with difficult decisions. He spins her a yarn about needing space. He tells her he's going to Portugal on a short break with his mates. He assures her everything will be fine and that he'll call as soon as he gets back. But already, before he even leaves, his eye is roving. To the source of the giddy laughter, rolling across the bar. To the pretty blonde, in the circle of friends, having a good time. To Sarah . . .

Sarah Jane Boost was a regular at the Bull and though I'd noticed her there several times, with a group we called 'the under-fives' because of how young they were, we had never actually spoken. I invited them to join us for a drink, and Sarah and I paired off at the end of the night to a disco bar near Eltham, and began dating regularly when I returned from Portugal and ended my relationship with Joanne. Sarah was seventeen, five years younger than me, and worked in the city as a runner in the Stock Exchange. She was good-looking rather than stunning, but what really set her apart was the unique sense of humour she inherited from her mother, Pauline. On the day she first invited me home, there was a ribbon across the gate, and her parents emerged with scissors as we stepped from the car. A few weeks later, we were shopping one afternoon in the High Street in Bromley, when Pauline spotted us from a bus stop across the road. I was just about to wave hello when she turned to the other commuters and started gesturing in my direction.

'Look,' she gasped.

'It's him,' she gasped.

'Over there!' she gasped.

'It's Tony Cascarino!'

And they all looked across and started scratching their heads: 'Tony who?' It was embarrassing.

Sarah, thankfully, wasn't quite as abrasive and could really make me laugh. We used to bounce off each other like a double act and Sarah was always the life and soul of the party when we were out. After a few months, we started living together and the next two years were the happiest of our lives. In hindsight, when I think about it now, this was probably because essentially nothing had changed. Although, technically, we were living together, when you added up the time we spent in each other's company, we were still living separate lives. On weekdays, while Sarah was either working late or out with her friends, I was either training or playing cards or out with mine. One day, about a year after she'd moved in, I was watching telly in the front room of the house, when it suddenly dawned that we had never actually sat in the room together. Or spent time, other than sleeping, together in the house. But what did it matter, when we were happy? And we *were* happy. And in November of '87 we became engaged.

Why? I don't know. It certainly wasn't planned. There was no candlelight dinner. I did not go down on my knee. It just seemed a logical progression. We were living together and getting on well and came home from an afternoon's shopping with two rings, like a million couples before us. I can't honestly say we were head-over-heels in love but then, how honest can I be, given the bitterness that now divides us and everything that's happened since? Hindsight isn't always 20/20 vision. Of course we were in love. We had to be in love. We did the things lovers do. We had a song, 'You and I,' our own love anthem, written for us specially by Stevie Wonder.

So what was I doing, gazing out on a south Dublin graveyard, six weeks before I was due to be wed? I was acting the scorpion, that's what. I was doing what scorpions do, when it's late and they've had a drink and a good-looking lady scorpion offers them the chance to flex their tail. But though I certainly enjoyed the moment, the aftermath wasn't fun. Sarah called me at the hotel next day.

'So, what did you get up to last night, then? Have a good time?'

'Naah, not much, just went for a drink with a couple of the lads.'

It was the first time I'd been with anyone else since we'd met.

I slept in my mother's house on the night of Friday, 8 July, and awoke next morning and stared at the ceiling. Later that afternoon, I would walk down the aisle with Sarah but my brief encounter in Dublin was still bothering me. Was I doing the right thing?

'Forget about it, Tony, it's just big day nerves. Everyone feels that way.'

'Bollocks! You cheated and you know it! You're not even married but you're already playing the field.'

'It was just a one-off, a last-minute fling.'

'Yeah, sure.'

'It won't happen again.'

'How could you do that to someone you purport to love?'

'I do love her!'

'Of course you do.'

'And anyway, I was still a single man.'
'Fine, you're right, I'm sure Sarah will understand.'

Having lived through the misery of my parents' split, I did not want my marriage to go the same way, and that my mother and sister also harboured doubts added to my anxiety. Neither Mandy nor my mother had ever really taken to Sarah and though they'd never said anything, I suspected, deep down, that they were worried I was making a mistake. But there was a side to Sarah that never came out in public: a warm, generous and sensitive side they had never seen. And any doubts *I* had about the wedding weren't about Sarah at all; they were about me.

I lazed around for a while after breakfasting with Mum, then slipped down to the Bull with my best man, Peter Cappuccio, for a lunchtime drink. Most of the friends I had grown up with were there and five pints later – 'You have to be fit to drink' – we were all in flying form. I was still without a tie for my suit, so we made a frantic dash to Bexley and found a reasonably presentable match, then showered, changed and raced to Chislehurst, where Peter got me to the church on time. Sarah, meanwhile, was taking everything in her stride. When I enquired, later, 'What the bleedin' 'ell kept you?' she informed me with a grin that when the chauffeur had arrived, she'd invited him to join her for a whisky and cigar on the lawn. A touch zany perhaps, but the girl definitely had class. The reception went well. Sarah's family were Millwall supporters and with most of the team present, a great night was had by all. Between signing autographs and talking football, I hardly saw Sarah until the last dance. But the last dance was nice. They played our song.

We honeymooned in Paris and Corsica and before the end of the trip we were haggling like we'd been married for years. It was mostly harmless stuff. In Paris, Sarah threw a wobbly when I suggested we stay in our hotel room and ignore the lure of the city to watch the Tour de France . . . which, I suppose, was fair enough. And in Corsica, while I was content to sit in the lobby each evening playing Trivial Pursuit, Sarah wanted to paint the town . . . which would have been fair enough had there been a town to paint! Unfortunately, the resort we had chosen was beautiful, but remote. But there were some good moments too, and we returned home looking forward not so much to the 'challenge of our new life together' but to just carrying on where we'd left off. With her doing her thing and me doing mine. With the training and the cards and the games and the restaurants and the waking on Sunday morning/ afternoon – 'Hi, I'm Tony,' 'Hi, I'm Sarah' – bombed from Saturday night.

And for fourteen months, that's mostly how it was. My first season in Division One went brilliantly. I buried a ghost and (twice!) put the ball past Neville Southall at Everton; replaced Frank Stapleton as Jack's first choice and hit the post at Anfield, my childhood theatre of dreams. Things were happening for me. I was playing the best football of my life. My star was in the incline. And then, Michael was born.

What if we were born with the ability to record every single moment of our waking lives? What if we retained crystal-clear images of every face we'd ever seen from the moment we opened our eyes? What if we remembered the exchanges between our parents when we were screaming late at night? Who changed us. Who wouldn't. Where we lived. How we slept. Our first conscious thought. Would we ever speak to our fathers again? I'm not sure Michael would.

He was born on Friday, 22 September 1989. I remember it because it was a Friday and the following afternoon we beat Sheffield Wednesday at the Den and I scored my third goal of the season. I remember it because it was four months after we had beaten Hungary in a World Cup qualifying game in Dublin and I had cheated on Sarah again. I remember it because two weeks later I scored a goal against Northern Ireland and was playing so well that Alex Ferguson offered £2 million for me at Christmas. I remember it because he was born at a time in my life when I was infected with the disease of 'me'. My feelings. My needs. My world. Me.

Michael brought responsibility I didn't want to know about. Michael was Sarah's idea. She had lost her job in the 1989 Crash and was spending more time at home, and a baby seemed a logical progression. Sarah made all the sacrifices. Michael's birth changed nothing for me. I continued driving to the card school after training and continued staying out late with my mates and continued to do whatever made me happy. That's when the arguments *really* started. I was, according to Sarah, a horrible selfish bastard. I denied it, of course, and fought my corner, but there was no defence.

Six months later, in March 1990, we moved north to Birmingham, when I accepted an offer to play for Aston Villa. For me, it was the shot at the big time I'd been waiting for. For us, it was the chance to start again. We bought a nice house in Sutton Coldfield and cut adrift from the card school and the other temptations of London, and we began to spend time with each other again. My first six games for Villa weren't hectic but relations with Sarah definitely improved. The World Cup finals were just around the corner, the summit before the fall . . .

Chapter Ten
Scent of a Winner

Look at the Irish. They sing and none of them know the words. Jack sings, and all he knows is 'Blaydon Races' and 'Cushy Butterfield.' But look at the pride they have in those green shirts.

– Lawrie McMenemy

The logic of worldly success rests on a fallacy: the strange error that our perfection depends on the thoughts and opinions and applause of other men! A weird life it is, indeed, to be living always in somebody else's imagination, as if that were the only place in which one could at last become real!
– Thomas Merton, The Seven Storey Mountain

A few months before we left for Birmingham and Aston Villa, John Docherty, my manager at Millwall, called me into his office one afternoon, in foul mood. The team was struggling and he was starting to feel the strain.

'We're giving you a green shirt on Saturday,' he spat.

'What do you mean?' I asked.

'We're going to send you out on Saturday in fucking green.'

'I'm sorry, boss,' I said. 'I'm not with you.'

'I watched the game last Wednesday and saw the running you did for Ireland and then you play for us on Saturday and you're a lump of fucking shit! So we're sending you out in green this week. I want you to play for us like you played for them.'

'No, boss, you're wrong,' I argued. 'The shirt has nothing to do with it.'

102

But later, when I gave it some thought, I had to concede that he was right: all my best performances that season had been for Ireland. But was that really so unusual? I mean, what was Docherty's problem? Wasn't it the most natural thing in the world to raise your game for your country? Except that Ireland wasn't my country. I wasn't Irish, as I'll explain later. It wasn't patriotism. I wasn't doing it for the flag. Was there something about Jack Charlton that was bringing out the best in me?

My relationship with Jack got off to a shaky start, that summer in '88. By shadow boxing with Kevin Sheedy (Jack had a thing about him) in my first training session, I hadn't exactly taken the express route to his heart. However my goal against Poland soon redressed the balance and I was delighted to secure the last remaining place in the squad for the European Championships in Germany. We prepared for the finals at a training camp in Dublin and though I wasn't centrally involved, I used my time on the periphery of the team to observe the manager and how he worked. The key to a harmonious relationship with Jack, I quickly learned, was to understand a few basic principles. Well, actually, there was just one basic principle. The manager's instructions weren't open to interpretation. The dressing room wasn't a forum for debate. Jack never pretended he was running a democracy. When he said, 'Jump,' you asked, 'How high?'

I remember a World Cup qualifying game against Spain once, when he ordered John Sheridan, who was playing midfield, not to lose possession by playing short passes to either me or John Aldridge up front. 'I don't want you giving it to the centre forward's feet and playing cute one-twos,' he was told. 'If you do it, I'll pull you off.' I was standing next to John when he was given the order and knew from the tone of Jack's voice that if he tried it even once, he'd be off. So did John. He was absolutely terrified. This, after all, was the same manager who had substituted the great Liam Brady ten minutes before half time in his last appearance for Ireland in a friendly against West

Germany at Lansdowne Road. I was sitting on the bench when he made the decision and though he knew it wouldn't endear him to the crowd, he wasn't changing his mind. 'I know it's Brady's day,' he bellowed, 'but there's a World Cup to prepare for and I've got to get the midfield right! The Germans are running riot!' He was ruthless in the heat of competition, but this wasn't the only factor in the way he transformed the team.

He was a funny man, as funny as I have known, and had a great ability to tell stories and see the comic side of life. In June '88, a week before we left for Germany, he organized a trip to the races one afternoon where, after a couple of punts and a couple of pints, we all soon forgot the numbing dullness of the training camp. As a mark of appreciation (and, it's fair to say, in the hope we might be allowed another drink), we began singing his praises on the journey back to the hotel.

> 'We love you Jack-ie, we do,
> We love you Jack-ie, we do,
> We love you Jack-ie, we do,
> Oh, Jackie we love you . . .'

At first, he pretended not to buy it: 'Shut up! Don't try all that rubbish with me. You're not fucking stopping at a pub for a pint. You lot are going straight back to the hotel.' But five minutes later, there was a huge cheer when the bus pulled into a hostelry by the side of the road. 'OK, everybody off,' he smiled, 'but let's be clear on one thing: *I am not buying the drinks!*' As an exercise in building team spirit it was brilliant. And if there was one quality the team possessed in abundance it was spirit.

Euro '88 was a great experience. At first, we were perceived as the pub team of the tournament – a happy-go-lucky bunch, who partied with their supporters and were just happy to be involved. But when we beat England in our opening game and were unlucky to concede a draw to the Soviet Union, we began to be taken seriously. I sat on the bench for both those games and didn't get to play until the last eight minutes of our narrow defeat to Holland, but thoroughly enjoyed just being with the squad. We had a great card school going and by the end of the tournament, a lot of money had been won and lost. Aldo (John Aldridge) and Dave Kelly had taken a hammering; Kevin Moran and Liam Brady were even; but Niall and I were ahead and looking forward to pocketing our winnings, when Liam suddenly announced that, 'in the spirit of the occasion and the interests of team morale', all debts were off. I thought, 'You can't do that! I've won a right few quid!' But Liam was right. It had been a memorable week. The team was more important.

Three months later, the first of the qualifying games for World Cup '90 began in Belfast. I hit the post and played well in our scoreless draw with Northern Ireland. Jack had handed me Frank Stapleton's role and wanted me to play as a target man who dropped into midfield when we didn't have the ball. I found it difficult at first but gradually became more confident and before the end of the campaign had established myself as one of the cornerstones of the team. In November '89, after successive victories over Spain, Hungary and Northern Ireland, we travelled to Valetta, needing a result against Malta to secure a place in the finals for the first time in history. We were joined in our quest by thousands of fans who had made the trip from Ireland and our joy was unrestrained when we won 2–0. We celebrated in Valetta after the game and I eventually ended up in a disco bar with Andy Townsend, Ray Houghton and at least a thousand supporters. John Aldridge was also part of our group but went missing as soon as we reached the bar.

'Where's Aldo?' I asked.

'He's in 'ere somewhere,' Ray replied.

'There he is!' Andy announced, 'Fuckin' 'ell!' And when we looked to where he was pointing, the prostrate body of Ireland's two-goal hero – his first in twenty games – was being ferried over the heads of the sea of supporters on the dance floor, on a conveyor belt of hands. 'Can you imagine that happening in any other country?' Andy observed. He was right. In England, they'd have been thumping him.

Italia '90 wasn't my first visit to the World Cup finals. In the summer of '82, I had travelled with some friends to Spain and watched England play Germany in Madrid. Although I had just signed for Gillingham, I never imagined that I would one day return to the finals as a player. And if someone had suggested that not only would I play but I would line out against England, I'd have advised them to consult their shrink. How could I play against England? I'd supported England as a boy; England was my team, the land of my birth. But that's exactly what transpired: eight years later, on a wet and windy night in Cagliari, I walked out for my country, to face my country, in the biggest game of my career. And I wasn't alone. Six of the team wearing green that night were born in England. A seventh, Ray Houghton, was born in Glasgow. Our manager, Jack Charlton, was one of the most famous English footballers of all time! But there was no question of divided loyalties for any of us. On the contrary, it made us even hungrier to succeed because although we never pretended we were 100 per cent Irish, we were 100 per cent committed to Ireland and its team.

I was playing against Terry Butcher, one of the world's best defenders. I was the most nervous I have ever been before a game but I was quietly confident, as I'd worked hard during the build-up and played reasonably well. England scored first with a goal from Gary Lineker in the ninth minute, and Kevin Sheedy put us back in it with a great strike midway through the second half. It was a scrappy game, played in horrible conditions, and though I acquitted myself reasonably well, I had one horrible moment at the end when Butcher slipped in behind me at the far post and headed into the side netting from a free kick out left. There was nothing Jack despised more than sloppy marking and I thought I was in for a right bollocking after the game. But 1–1 was a better result for us than for them, and in the elation of the dressing room, my error was overlooked.

A week later we travelled to Palermo to play Egypt, who were perceived as the soft touch of the group. This, the experts lectured, was a game we had to win. And to be fair, we weren't arguing, but we failed to ignite on a boiling Sunday afternoon and were forced to settle for another draw. Two days later, Jack organized a practice game and began toying with options for the final group game against Holland. He was still crusty and irritable after the Egypt performance and I was aware, running out, of the need to look sharp. But from the moment the session began, I was a disaster and missed chance after chance. I could hear Jack barking on the sideline, 'Look at 'im! He's gone! His fucking confidence is gone!'

Which, to me, sounded ridiculous.

'You're fucked. He thinks your confidence has gone.'

'Bollocks.'

'Are you sure?'

'Of course I'm fucking sure, I'm just having one of those days.'

How many goals have you scored since signing for Villa?'

'Two.'

'In how many games?'

'Ten.'

'You're not going to tell me that Jack hasn't noticed?'

'Yeah, but I've been playing well for Ireland.'

'And you haven't felt threatened lately by the blazing form of Niall?'

'Look, for fuck's sake, it was obviously something I ate at breakfast! A bad day at the office! They happen to everyone in every walk of life.'

But Jack didn't see it quite that way. Halfway through the session, he ordered me to switch with Niall, who immediately looked sharper and began to score. Later that afternoon, when the team to play Holland was announced, I was named as one of the substitutes. Furious, I called Jack aside to confront him about his decision.

'Give me one good reason why you've left me out,' I

demanded. 'In all the games I've played for you, I haven't let
you down once! You said yourself, after the . . .'

But Jack wasn't listening. His face had turned crimson. 'You
were fucking crap!' he exploded. And then he started reaming
off a litany of mistakes and I realized that nothing I could say
would change his mind.

Gutted, I went for a walk and shed a few tears but couldn't
face the lads at mealtime. Kevin Moran thought it hilarious:
'That's the first time I've ever heard of anyone being dropped
because of a training session,' he laughed. But it was more than
just a 'dropping'. Here's a record of my next nine appearances
for Ireland:

- v. Holland (0–0), June 1990. Subs: Cascarino for Aldridge (62 mins)
- v. Rumania (0–0), June 1990. Subs: Cascarino for Aldridge (22 mins)
- v. Italy (0–1), June 1990. Subs: Cascarino for Quinn (52 mins)
- v. Morocco (1–0), September 1990. Subs: Cascarino for Quinn (59 mins)
- v. Turkey (5–0), October 1990. Subs: Cascarino for Quinn (68 mins)
- v. England (1–1), November 1990. Subs: Cascarino for Quinn (61 mins)
- v. England (1–1), March 1991. Subs: Cascarino for Aldridge (72 mins)
- v. Poland (0–0), May 1991. Subs: Cascarino for Quinn (71 mins)
- v. Chile (1–1), May 1991. Subs: Cascarino for Sheedy (70 mins)

And for the next five years, as long as Jack had Niall as an
option, that's how it was. As long as Jack had the option of
Niall, I was second-rate. And nothing – not my goal against
England in Dublin, or my winner against Germany in the
summer of '94, or some of my great performances later at

Marseilles – was ever enough to change his mind. For stepping out of bed on the wrong side that morning, I was effectively sentenced to life on the bench. Do I resent him for it? Do I recount the story through gritted teeth? Not at all. He definitely upset me and it certainly wasn't fair, but how can I ignore what made him great?

Four years later, on a night off during our training camp in Orlando before World Cup '94, I met a girl at a bar in Church Street and invited her back to the team hotel. For security reasons, access to the team floor was restricted to team personnel, but I managed to divert the guards for long enough for my friend to slip into the room.

Things were progressing nicely when we were suddenly interrupted by a commotion outside. The police had arrived and were checking all the rooms.

'What's the problem?' I asked, when the knock came on the door.

'The cameras have picked up an intruder,' the officer replied. 'Seen anything?'

'Not a thing,' I said.

The search continued but the intruder wasn't found.

The following morning at training, Jack gathered us in a circle. 'Who was the fucker with the bird in his room?' he demanded. 'Come on, own up.' He seemed reasonably calm at first but grew visibly more irritable with every negative response.

'Andy?'

'No way, Jack.'

'Was it you, Aldo?'

'No, Jack, it definitely wasn't me.'

'Stan?'

'Nope.'

'Jason [McAteer]?'

'No Jack.'

'Raymond?'

'No.'

'Roy?'

'Naah.'

One by one, he put the question to almost everyone in the group but me. I couldn't believe it. Had he confused the inquisition with the naming of his team? Anyway, by the time he was finished, he was *really* pissed.

'Right! If that's the way it's going to be, fine. But don't think you're going to get away with it! I'll find the bastard whoever he is and when I do he'll fucking regret it!'

Dismissed, we broke off and began to warm up, but before I'd reached the corner of the pitch, my conscience was at me and I decided to own up.

'What's up?' he asked.

'It was me, Jack,' I mumbled.

'What do you mean?'

'It was me. I brought the girl back to the room.'

He completely lost the head. 'What! We're training for the fucking World Cup and you take a bird back to the room!'

A group of journalists had moved into range. I thought, For fuck's sake, Jack, keep your voice down. We don't want them to get wind of it. But how do you tell Jack Charlton to shut it when he's frothing from the mouth with rage?

'I'm really sorry, Jack,' I grovelled. ' I promise, this will never happen again.'

But there was no calming the storm.

'I should fucking send you home,' he raged.

Now the possibility of being sent home in disgrace wasn't, I must admit, something I'd considered when deciding to come clean. I thought: 'Fuck! You stupid bastard! He's going to make an example of you! He's going to send you home before you've even had a kick!' I stood, in silence, awaiting judgement.

He grumbled and continued to seethe until at last it was delivered: 'Well, I hope she was fucking worth it!' he exploded. And that was it. That's how it ended. We looked at each other and started laughing and it was never mentioned again.

SCENT OF A WINNER

Two years ago, when Teddy Sheringham was exposed by the tabloids for drinking at a disco, a week before the start of France '98, he was made to read a letter of apology before the cameras by the England manager, Glenn Hoddle. I remember watching it on TV, and feeling bad for Teddy and the humiliation he had to endure. I also remember thinking of Jack and what he'd have done. He'd have said, 'Of course he had a drink. I told him to have a drink. He's been training non-stop for three weeks! Do you think I'm going to keep him locked up? He'd be bored out of his mind. There's a week before the tournament starts and we're back training tomorrow, so where's the problem?' And then, after making his little speech, he would have taken Teddy behind closed doors and given him the biggest bollocking of his life. Jack understood that your team was your family, and you didn't expose your family and expect to retain their respect.

And that's why he was never 'Charlton' to me, always 'Jack'. And that's why I continued to answer, whenever he called. For sure, out on the pitch, we did it for ourselves, but we also did it for Jack, no question. In my eighteen years in football, he was easily the best I've known.

But I digress. We were about to play Holland and I had just been dropped and in my rush to explain why Jack was God, I fast forwarded too quickly and neglected to explain how we became kings. Now we must rewind to the Dutch game. And the Dutch goal. And Niall's equalizer. And the 1–1 draw that allowed us to progress to the second phase of the tournament. And the penalty shoot-out with Rumania that kick-started us into the fast lane and an amazing period in our lives . . .

The game was played on a boiling hot afternoon in Genoa. After two hours of stalemate, we collapsed on the pitch in varying states of distress. Jack walked on and told us that whatever happened in the next few minutes we had done the country proud. We were looking down the barrel of a penalty shoot-out. Five volunteers were required. 'Right,' Ray

FULL TIME

Houghton, announced, 'who fancies it?' There was no immediate response.

Neither of our two designated specialists – Aldo or Ronnie Whelan – had finished the game, which put the onus on Kevin Sheedy, who promptly agreed to take the first. Ray volunteered, and so did Andy and Dave O'Leary, but then there was an uneasy pause. Paul McGrath clearly wasn't having it and walked away. We were one short of the quota. Suddenly, inevitably, the spotlight turned to me.

'What about it, Cass?' Ray asked, exasperated. 'Are you a man or a fucking mouse?'

'Mouse,' Andy sniggered, and walked away.

'Yeah, I'll have one,' I said.

There was no way out.

The Rumanians won the toss and had the advantage of shooting first. Kevin, Ray and Andy had all passed the test with honour and we were 4–3 down when I placed the ball on the spot. I could hear the fans behind the goal chanting my name; and my heart thumping in my chest; and the voice, as ever, sowing the seeds of doubt.

'You look like a man about to meet a firing squad.'

'I'm not listening.'

'Or Neville Southall.'

'Piss off.'

'Did you notice how big the goalie was when you placed the ball?'

'I did, actually.'

'The whole world is watching. Frightening, isn't it?'

'I'm a professional. I can handle it.'

'Really? You'd better assure your mother. "Don't do it son!" she's screaming. "What happens if you miss?"'

My legs felt like rubber sticks as I ran towards the ball. I choked over the shot and stubbed my toe in the turf on contact and almost fainted with relief as the ball followed the divot, under the keeper's arm and into the back of the net. It was a terrible penalty but Lady Luck had been kind to me and when

112

Dave converted the final kick after a brilliant save by Packie, the mother of all celebrations began. We had reached the quarter finals of the World Cup.

Five days later, our great adventure ended with a 1–0 defeat to Italy in Rome. On the morning after the game, we boarded a flight for Dublin, where a champagne reception at the airport was followed by a ticker-tape parade into the city on an open-top bus, where an estimated quarter of a million people lined the streets to welcome us home. It was quite extraordinary. In the seven months since we'd qualified for the finals, the country had been ravaged by the most contagious fever since the foundation of the state. Football fever. Blotched in green, white and orange, we could not have been greeted more fervently if we'd won! And on that hot summer afternoon in June, there was no greater celebrity than to play for the team that Jack built. We were Masters of the Universe. Kings.

Sarah was with me on the coach that afternoon. She enjoyed the status of being married to a footballer but, like most of the wives, had become uneasy with the attention we were getting in Dublin and the trappings of success. One afternoon, whilst out shopping in the city, she overheard two store assistants gossiping about the team: '. . . and Cascarino, well, he's the Italian stallion!' I laughed it off when she mentioned it on her return and swore I'd never set foot in the place, but I know she was concerned. And with good reason. In London, I could go shopping or take the tube or walk the streets in almost total anonymity. In Dublin, I was recognised by every man, woman and child. Six thousand people turned up to meet me one afternoon when I arrived to open a fête in Tipperary. I thought the engagement would take about an hour at most but I was absolutely mobbed – 'Sign this, Tony', 'Well done, Tony' – and by the end of the day, had to beg to get away. They just couldn't get enough of me. And everywhere we went it was the same.

Nightclubs were offering us appearance fees and free drink for the night. We'd arrive and be sectioned off in a corner, and by the end of the night there'd be a thousand people on our side of the rope and about ten outside. And there was never any rowdiness or aggression shown to us when we mingled – it was just a real fun time. I remember our first game after the World Cup, a friendly against Morocco at Dalymount Park. As we were walking out to warm up, Jack tapped me on the shoulder: 'Listen to my ovation,' he smiled. And when he raised his arm, the place just erupted. He loved the way the people had embraced his team. There were very few withdrawals from the squad in those days. Players were turning up injured, just to be involved in the group, which was hardly a surprise when you considered some of the privileges.

When we weren't opening shops, modelling clothes or doing fashion shoots for magazines, we were fending off girls, literally queuing to be screwed by one of the 'boys in green'. They'd call our rooms, pretending they were wives or girl-friends, and it got to a stage where there was just no escape and the phone was left permanently off the hook. Some handled it better than others and resisted the temptations: I tried to stay onside but more often than not succumbed. It was just so ridiculously easy. It didn't matter whether we were nice to them or behaved like complete wankers, they just wanted to be straddled by one of the champions; we were trophies they could exhibit to their friends.

Success isn't pretty when you see what it does to people up close. Five years later, in the summer of '95, I was rooming with Andy at an hotel in Limerick, when the folly of it all hit home. We had just returned from training and were about to descend for lunch when we heard some girls screaming from the garden beneath our window. I opened the window and gave them a wave and for a moment, just a moment, it was just like old times.

'Aghhhh! Tony! Tony!' they squealed. But then they immediately went and spoiled it: 'Where's Jason and Gary and Phil?' In the five years since Italia '90, the 'three amigos' – Jason McAteer, Gary Kelly and Phil Babb – had brushed the oldies aside and taken over as the team's star trophies.

'What! Do you not want me or Andy any more?' I shouted, deciding to play along.

But we had obviously passed our sell-by date. They wanted Barabbas, all three of him, but Jason and Gary and Phil had gone to lunch.

'Can you throw us something from their room?' they cried.

Andy laughed and shook his head; I slipped next door and found a sweat-stained, skid-marked training slip on the floor. 'The only thing I could find is this!'

They started screaming hysterically. Instinctively, I threw the slip from the window and watched in amazement as the winner emerged triumphantly from the short stampede and scrum. She was holding the skid-marked shorts to her face! She was inhaling them like a scented handkerchief! I couldn't have made her happier if I'd dropped a million pounds! I thought: 'Fuck! What have I done?' And in that moment it was all there in front of me. The craving we have to be someone. The magnetic lure of fame.

Chapter Eleven
Contempt

'*So will your relationship with Packie Bonner and Chris Morris change now?*'

'*No, nothing will change.*'

'*Except that they'll have to call you boss, right?*'

'*No, I would hope they will call me Liam.*'

> – Liam Brady, the newly appointed manager of Glasgow Celtic, meets the press at Parkhead in June of '91

The supporters really gave us some stick. Really vicious. I was walking off the pitch when I caught the eye of this big fat guy who stands just beside the tunnel. He goes to reserve games, everything. I've seen him all over the country. He seems really aggressive. I've never spoken to him but I don't like him. I caught his eye and he gave me the old wanking sign. Contempt.

> – Eamon Dunphy, *Only a Game?*

All along the path we take in life there are signposts pointing the way. Four years ago, on the night I first met Nancy's manager Laszlo Boloni and decided I would leave Marseilles, I was sitting in the stands at the Parc des Princes in Paris, watching Nancy play Paris St Germain, when my attention was drawn to the game's outstanding player. Stephane Capiaux, a 25-year-old winger from Lille, was running around players as if they were standing still. He wasn't just single-handedly beating PSG; he was ripping them to shreds. I couldn't believe he was playing for Nancy! There had to be some mistake! It was one of the most gifted displays I had ever seen.

A week later we were team mates and a slightly different picture began to emerge. A brilliant, natural talent who had come late to the game, Stephane could do things with a ball that only great players can do. He talked like one of the best players in the world, and walked like one of the best players in the world and drove the same brand of car as the best players in the world. But would never be one of the best players in the world because of the basic flaw in his game.

In my eighteen years in football, he is the only team mate I ever grabbed by the throat and wanted to throttle after a game. We had been leading 2–0 in a game we desperately had to win against Laval, when he came off the bench late in the second half and handed them a point after being caught, twice, over-doing the flash. Stephane didn't understand the simple way to play. Incredibly inconsistent, he had no grasp at all of the basics of the game. And when his contract expired at the end of the season, it was no great surprise to any of us that Laszlo showed him the door. He got a decent move to (ironically enough) Laval, spent most of his year's salary on a flash new Mercedes, but was unlucky and spent most of the season sidelined with injury.

He popped into our dressing room the other night after our game with Marseilles. We chatted for a while and exchanged pleasantries. He's thirty-one now, and playing for Niort, who are currently fourth from bottom of the second division, but you'd never know it to look at him. He still dresses like a star, and still drives the Mercedes, and still dreams about a big move to England. I sincerely hope he gets it, but time is running out. It runs out for all of us in the end . . .

That's what Dick Tydeman tried to tell me when I was starting out at Gillingham. That's the advice I tried to give Stephane. 'Forget the flash cars,' I said. 'Buy an apartment! Invest in property! Work your bollocks off and make the most of what you have! Because tomorrow you'll wake up and it will be gone.' I was the signpost pointing the way. He should have looked at me, still scrimping and saving after a lifetime with some of the biggest clubs in the game, and thought: There's a lesson here for me.' But then, who was I to lecture? Didn't I once ignore the signposts? Wasn't I once exactly the same?

Liam Brady became my agent in the winter of '89. His long and illustrious career had finished in the shadows at West Ham and he'd abandoned his tracksuit for some fine Italian threads and a partnership in a sports management company called Drury Communications. I had never had much time for agents but had no hesitation when Liam offered to take me on board. Three months later I became a member of that (once) elite band known as the 'million-pound player' when I joined Aston Villa.

It was all set up for me when I returned from the World Cup to my first full season at Villa. All the signposts were pointing the same way: Twenty-seven years old, choice health, good knees, world-class agent – there was no conceivable way I could fail. But I managed to find one, and instead of moving forward the season was the start of a long and almost terminal decline. Now it can be argued that nine goals from thirty-six league appearances hardly constitutes failure. And it can be argued that I would have scored more had Josef Venglos, who had come in to replace Graham Taylor as manager, employed a game more suited to my strengths. But the bottom line really is that I had only myself to blame. Becoming a million-pound player was the worst thing that ever happened to me. With no John Docherty to stoke my fire and whip my arse into shape, I became lazy and complacent. I was a star. I was a million-pound player. The daily grind of the training ground didn't apply any more. When Saturday came I would just pull on my boots and perform.

A knee injury early in the season didn't help. I put on weight, lost my edge, and started to feel the lash from the fans.
'You useless wanker, Cascarino.'

'That was fucking shit.'

I could have halted the slide by addressing the nub of the problem: I should have spent the summer of '91 being determined to start my second season at the club, in the best physical shape of my life. But when you're young and immature, you don't often read the signs and when the opportunity arose to join Celtic in July, I let my heart rule my head and turned left when I should have turned right. And why not? Celtic, after all, was an Irish club and I was an Irish star. The fans would appreciate me, the league was a joke, and my friend and agent Liam Brady had just been appointed manager. How could I go wrong? So we moved north to Glasgow and rented a house that backed on to a golf course in the leafy suburb of Bothwell. And a litany of horrors began . . .

The Celtic job was a huge gamble for Liam. He had played with the best, and learnt from the best, but had no previous experience in managing a team. On the day I signed we went horse racing together in Hamilton. Although he was no longer my agent, it wasn't possible to just stop being friends and though inevitably there would be friction at some stage during the season, we didn't envisage any problem in this regard. I was his first, and in many ways, most important signing as a manager and he had broken the club record (£1.1 million) to take me to the club. Liam was always deep, always a thinker; and unlike Jack, who was as easy to read as a headline in the tabloids, it was sometimes hard to gauge what was going on in his head. He wanted us to address him by his first name, because Liam was classier than 'gaffer' or 'boss' and that's the way they did it on the Continent. He also encouraged us to pass the ball and play with style. But this was hardly a surprise. How else could a team managed by Brady play?

Our first game of the season was away to Dundee on 10 August. I'd lost a chunk of pre-season training with the hassle of moving house and started at least a half-stone overweight. The supporters gave me a great reception and I responded by really putting myself about until half-time, when I was forced to retire with a spasm in my back. It wasn't a brilliant début, but it wasn't a bad one either. We won 4–3 and then beat Dunfermline and Falkirk in our next two games. The mood in the camp was buoyant until the visit of Rangers and the first serious test of Liam's reign.

I'd heard a lot about the Old Firm game over the years and of the rivalry that exists between the Celtic and Rangers supporters, but it's only when you live in the city and see it up close that the true extent of the bigotry and hatred hits home. The ground was packed to capacity before we even stepped off the coach. And the atmosphere inside was unbelievable. The fans were frothing at the mouth and at each other's throats right through the warm-up. When we marched out to kick off, it really got intense.

Three weeks had passed since my début and I still hadn't scored. My milkman was a Celtic fan: 'Nae you worry, big mon.' So was the man who delivered our post: 'The form'll come big, mon, you're doin' fine.' But suddenly, the moment had come for *me* to deliver. There was no better way of endearing yourself to the Parkhead faithful (and insuring the essentials in life like fresh milk and regular post) then to put one over on *them*, Rangers, the eternal rivals. But though we tried our nuts off for ninety minutes they were just too strong and won 2–0. A week later, we were held to a scoreless draw at home to St Mirren. A week after that, we were beaten by St Johnston 1–0. Suddenly the fans began to lose patience . . .

'Away back to London, ye big fucker ye!'

'Och, yer fucking useless mon!'

I had run out of credits.

Liam was starting to get concerned and left me on the bench for the next two games. One night, out of the blue, he phoned me at home and suggested we meet for a drink at a local pub. We found a quiet corner and reviewed the season for the best part of an hour. It was all very amicable. He said he was aware of the abuse I was taking from supporters but asked me to concentrate on the task in hand.

'You're not doing me any favours by feeling sorry for yourself, Tony. I want you to put your head down and fight for your place on the team.'

'You're right, Liam,' I said. 'I know I've let you down. I'll try to do my best and turn things around.'

A week later, we were drawing 1–1 with Hearts at home, when he ordered me off the bench. I was on for about a minute, when Tommy Coyne found an opening and played a lovely ball forward that put me through on a one-on-one. As I galloped towards the ball, the Hearts keeper was racing from his line to close me down. And one of their centre halfs was a yard behind and matching me stride for stride. It was a time for cool heads and steel nerves . . .

'*Oh fuck, Cass, not you again!*

'*Please, not now.*'

'*It's Priestfield revisited! Here comes Neville Southall!*'

Like the sweetly struck golf shot, you always know, from the moment of impact, when you've caught the ball just right and are about to find the target. And from the moment it left my foot, I was never as sure of anything in my life that I'd shanked the fucking thing wide. But then, by an incredible stroke of good fortune, the outstretched leg of the defender arrived a split second later from behind, and my wayward strike was deflected into the corner of the Hearts net.

'GOOOOOOOOOOOAAALLLLLLLLLLLLL!!!

'*Christ, Big Mon, you've scored!*'

'*Fuck! I have.*'

Relief flooded over me as I accepted the hugs from my team mates and acknowledged the cheers from the fans. The nightmare was over. I had finally done it. I had finally managed to score. I jogged back to the halfway line and prepared for the restart. A minute later, I was just jumping to flick on a Packie Bonner clearance with the Hearts defender, Craig Levein, when I caught him with my elbow. Apologizing immediately, I assured him it was an accident, but he brushed me away and started swearing at me profusely. The game resumed and another minute later, I ran to pick him up on the edge of our box, when Hearts were awarded a free. I could see he was still pissed as we jostled for position and knew he'd take a swipe the moment the ball was kicked. When it came, I slipped his punch then lashed back instinctively and floored him in the box. The referee had no option but to award a penalty and sent me off immediately, seven minutes after Liam had sent me on. I started the lonely walk to the dressing room, expecting to be jeered and whistled off the pitch, but incredibly, I was treated to a standing ovation.

'Well done, big mon.'

'Brilliant, big mon.'

I thought: Wait a minute! I've just given away a penalty! I've just been sent off! What are our supporters so happy about? But later, when it was explained to me that Hearts were the 'Rangers' of the two teams in Edinburgh (Hibernian being the 'Celtic' equivalent) the fog began to clear. Slowly, I was learning the rules of engagement; with every day that passed, I was becoming more familiar with the language of contempt . . . 'blue noses', 'huns', 'wee orange bastards'. Today's lesson was that there was only one thing better than scoring against the 'Huns', and that was scoring against the Huns and then smacking one in the mouth.

The goal papered the cracks for a couple of weeks but I continued to struggle with my form. After just three months, I had pretty much had my fill of the Scottish Premier League. Parkhead and Ibrox were magnificent theatres for football but neither of the Edinburgh grounds were anything to get excited about, and then you'd go to places like Falkirk and Airdrie and it was like playing in the lower leagues. The ongoing bullshit of the phoney war in the city was also wearing me down.

'Don't go to "that" bookies again. That's a blue-nose bookies – if they realize you play for Celtic you'll be stabbed.'

'You can't play golf at that club. That's a blue-nose golf club.

None of the Celtic lads go there.'

So you'd go to the 'tim' bookies and play golf at the 'tim' clubs and do your shopping at the 'tim' centres and be abused by the 'tim' supporters instead!

The final straw was when a couple of my team mates warned me off because 'it had been noticed' that I'd been drinking with the Rangers players, Terry Hurlock and Ally McCoist. Big fucking deal! The Rangers players were just footballers to me! Ally McCoist was a bloody nice bloke! Terry Hurlock had been a friend since our time at Millwall! What was the problem? Why did I have to hate them because they played for the 'other' side?

At the end of October, we travelled to Switzerland to play Neuchatel in the second round of the UEFA Cup. A week earlier, I'd scored for Ireland in a European championship qualifier in Poland and Liam picked me in the team for the first time in a month. I responded with possibly the worst performance of my career. It was one of those awful nights when anything that can go wrong does go wrong; and when I wasn't giving the ball away, I was tripping over myself . . .

'Dear oh dear, Cass.'

'I know.'

'Neuchatel just love you, mate.'

'Is it that bad?'

'Bad! You're an embarrassment! Poor Brady hasn't a blade of hair left on his head. Your team mates are convinced you've taken a bung. They're thinking: "Nobody can be this fucking bad!"'

Liam pulled me off early in the second half. We were hammered 5–1 and the fans had a real go as we walked from the pitch. Liam was incensed in the dressing room. His team had played shamefully. His first managerial signing was making a mockery of him.

'What the fuck is going on, Tony? You were a disaster! I've never seen you play so badly!'

'Yeah, I dunno . . . I just . . . I was just crap.'

It wasn't quite the response he expected. 'What!' he exploded. 'You're actually admitting it!'

'Yes,' I replied, 'I am. At this moment in time, I'm a bad player. I'm playing crap.'

'Well, that's fucking marvellous: I pay a million pounds for a player and three months later, he tells me he's crap! Thanks a fucking lot.'

I showered and changed and joined the rest of the team on the coach ride back to the hotel, where we drowned our disgust with a couple of beers. We were almost ready for a sing-song when Liam arrived back and discovered the party in full flow. He was sore and cranky and gave us an unmerciful bollocking. I waited until he had finished and, boosted by the litres of Heineken washing around in my veins, I volunteered courageously to defend the troops.

'Take it easy, boss,' I said. 'We're only having a drink.'

The look he gave me almost cut me in two.

'So it's "boss" now, is it? You've always called me Liam.' He turned and left the room and I immediately understood that our relationship would never be the same.

There were no more friendly get-togethers in the weeks that followed. Not even my goal in our 1–1 draw with Rangers was enough to repair the damage and all further meetings between us were conducted in his office. When my form continued to deteriorate, I suggested that playing with the reserves for a while would restore my confidence. He dismissed the idea at first, saying he hadn't spent a million to bolster his reserves, but then he relented and let me go. Life with the reserves was a sobering experience. At Hamilton, the dressing room was so small that I couldn't stand up without bumping my head on the ceiling but, removed from the hostility and pressures, choking me at Parkhead, I began to enjoy myself again.

At Christmas, word began to filter through about a possible move to Chelsea. Tommy Boyd, a defender Chelsea had signed from Motherwell the previous summer, hadn't settled and was keen to return to Scotland, and Andy Townsend, who was the

Chelsea captain at the time and enjoying the form of his life, was working overtime on my behalf to organize a swap. Liam seemed reluctant when the deal was motioned and wasn't sure that he wanted Boyd. But he had pretty much given up on me and knew I was desperate to leave.

In January, we travelled to play St Johnstone in the league and I remember playing pool in the players' lounge before the game, delighted to have been left out of the team. With the Chelsea move gathering momentum, the last thing I needed was a fresh slaughtering from the press after another bad performance. I had abandoned all hope of rescuing my reputation in Scotland. It was time to cut and run. In the first week of February, Liam called me into his office: 'We've agreed a swap with Chelsea. Tommy Boyd is coming up on Wednesday to discuss terms.' Two days later, Boyd arrived with Chelsea's financial director, Colin Hutchinson, and after protracted negotiations – *'Come on, Tommy! For fuck's sake sign the form!'* – the deal was done. Liam didn't say much. He didn't have to. Four goals was a poor return for his million-pound investment. We parted without shaking hands.

There was a photographer waiting in the car park when I stepped outside. He'd heard a rumour about the swap and had been hanging around for days. I'd had my fill of the Scottish press and wasn't overly fussed about having my exit from the club recorded and covered my head with a balaclava as I walked to the car. The bloke was a right bastard, really aggressive.

'Take it off,' he ordered, grabbing at the hat. 'I can't see your face.'

'Get fucked,' I said, brushing past.

On the way home I realized that the balaclava had been a mistake. I could just see the headline in the morning papers: 'SMASH AND GRAB! CASCARINO TAKES THE MILLION AND RUNS!' But by the time the first editions hit the stands, I was already halfway to London . . .

*

FULL TIME

Three days later, I made my début for Chelsea against Crystal Palace. There was no reaction at all when I was introduced to the crowd and it was obvious, before I had even kicked a ball, that my performances north of the border had not gone unnoticed. First impressions tend to be lasting with supporters. I thought: If ever you need a goal, old son, it's now. With four minutes to go, we were trailing 1–0 when I got on the end of a cross and half-volleyed past the keeper to score. And though they weren't chanting my name when it was over, I walked off the field to general, if not generous, applause. A point was a point.

Later that evening, I went out for a meal with Andy and his wife Jackie to a fashionable restaurant in West Kensington. I was still buzzing with adrenaline, and it felt great to be back in London again; great to have scored; great to be home. Ian Porterfield, the Chelsea manager, had given me a slap on the back in the dressing room. Ken Bates, the chairman, had also popped by to say well done. In the space of one game, it was as if everything had turned. Football was truly a wonderful game. Life was good; the garden was rosy; we would all live happily ever after. But within weeks, normal service had resumed. My knee was giving me grief; I was struggling with my weight; my confidence was rattled; I couldn't score. The goals dried up. There was no breathing space from the Chelsea supporters and by the end of the month the abuse was as bad as it had ever been in Glasgow.

'You useless wanker, Cascarino.'

'Get your finger out, you fat-arsed Irish cunt!'

Two months after scoring at my début, I scored my second for Chelsea in a 2–1 defeat of West Ham at Stamford Bridge. A week later, we were away to Leeds, and I was booed by the Chelsea supporters when my name was announced. Denis Wise couldn't believe it and started laughing his bollocks off: 'Oh they love you, don't they, Cass? Go on, give 'em a wave.'

Ken Bates was also having second thoughts. During an end-of-season tour to Canada, when informed that his manager was

126

thinking of signing Norwich's Robert Fleck, he barked, 'I don't want another fucking disaster like Cascarino.' Later, when he raised the issue again at a meeting with four of the club's most influential players – Andy, Denis Wise, Vinny Jones and Kerry Dixon – I was grateful for their support.

'He'll be fine when he sorts his knee out.'

'Just give him a bit of time.'

'Don't worry, Ken, he'll do it for you.'

'Cass is all right.'

Chelsea, it has to be said, was a very strange team at the time. Ian Porterfield was a good player in his day and a lovely man but the 'gang of four' had massive influence and used to give him an awful time. We trained near Heathrow airport and shortly after I had just joined the club I remember thinking Andy was in trouble when he arrived one morning thirty minutes late. 'Sorry, gaffer,' he grinned. 'The fucking M25 was murder this morning.' And that was it. He just carried on. Nothing was said. A few days later, Ian's suggestion that we 'do a bit of hard [physical] stuff' was greeted with uproar. 'Oh, fuck off! We're not doing that! Get the balls out! We're having a five-a-side!' And Ian just laughed and acquiesced.

The end-of-season tour to Canada was great fun. Dundee United had also been invited and were on the same flight to Vancouver. We arrived at the airport and picked up our bags, and noticed, on exiting the terminal, that there was just one coach waiting to take both teams to the hotel. 'I'm not getting into a bus with that lot,' Vinny Jones announced. 'They're fucking shite.' We looked at him and thought he was joking, but he was adamant he wasn't sharing the coach – 'Fucking Dundee' – and immediately commandeered a stretch limo that was parked fifty yards to the right. Vinny was very much the leader of the gang and could be ruthlessly cutting. Denis was 'the Rat', who enjoyed winding everyone up. Andy and Kerry were the jokers of the pack, two brilliant wits who lived for fun. And I was the whipping boy, just happy to be along for the ride. I followed them to the limo and jumped inside. On the journey to the hotel, we popped a bottle of bubbly and waved our glasses out of the window at the coach, travelling behind. I'm not sure what my team mates or the lads from Dundee made of it but I can hazard a guess . . .

'Fucking Cascarino!'

'Who the fuck does he think he is?'

'He was shite in Scotland!'

'He's shite in England!'

'Just fucking look at him.'

The word is contempt.

Robert Fleck arrived from Norwich at the start of the following season and the chairman's worst fears were realized. No matter what way you looked at it, two goals from thirty-one league appearances made him 'another fucking disaster', but I wasn't complaining because it took the heat off me. I pulled on the Chelsea shirt just nine times in the league and spent the year eating sandwiches and drinking beer in the stands, and going in and out to hospital to have my cartilage scraped. The whole season just seemed to drift by aimlessly. Ian Porterfield was sacked and replaced by Glenn Hoddle. It was the summer of '93 and after three years of tailspin, I had almost reached the endgame. There was one more year to run on my Chelsea contract.

I couldn't continue like this.

Chapter Twelve
The Truth about Laughing Gas

If every day a man takes orders in silence from an incompetent superior, if every day he solemnly performs ritual acts which he privately finds ridiculous, if he unhesitatingly gives answers to questionnaires which are contrary to his real opinions and is prepared to deny his own self in public, if he sees no difficulty in feigning sympathy or even affection where, in fact, he feels only aversion, it still does not mean that he has entirely lost the use of one of the basic human senses, namely, the sense of humiliation.

– Vaclav Havel, *Living in Truth*

The writing doesn't always stay motionless on the wall; sometimes it jumps out and slaps you on the face. I have known Peter Cappuccio all my life. We went to school together, he was my best man on the day I married Sarah, and his brother Tony is married to my sister, Mandy, which makes him as close to family as any friend can be. One Sunday afternoon, during the last days of Porterfield's regime as manager of Chelsea, we were sitting having a drink together, when he began complaining about an ongoing problem he was having at work – which would have been fine, if it hadn't related to an ongoing problem I was having at work.

'Are you going to liven up?' he enquired.

'How do you mean?' I asked.

'I'm taking so much stick, defending you from the Chelsea punters at work, that it's driving me fucking crazy!'

He knew, as soon as he said it, that I was hurt and apologized immediately. What he didn't know was that he had also done me a favour because, while I can't say the incident was a turning point, it was certainly a starting point. Maybe it's the nature of the game, but we always think of ourselves as the only people in the firing line. I'd never considered Peter at work or Michael, my ten-year-old son, at school, or what it was like to be the mother or sister or wife of 'fucking Cascarino'. And so, that summer of '93, during a two-week holiday with Sarah and the kids in Florida, I took to the roads and ran every day and resolved to turn things round.

When I close my eyes and think of Glenn Hoddle, two images spring to mind. The first is of Hoddle the player, and that incredible goal for Spurs, when he raced with the ball to the edge of the Watford box and chipped the goalkeeper when everyone expected him to cross. The second is of Hoddle the manager, on the morning Paul Elliot arrived in our dressing room wearing an immaculate leather trenchcoat and stood there, stunned, as Hoddle the manager raced to the 'cover' of a bin in the corner and started shooting him with imaginary bullets – 'Pshhhh', Pshhhh' – like a five-year-old with a cowboy pistol set. What Paul didn't realize was that Glenn was trying to be funny, and when Glenn tried to be funny it was time to pass round the laughing gas because he was probably the unfunniest man I have ever known. He was also completely besotted with himself.

On one of his first sessions in charge of Chelsea, he gathered us around one morning at the training ground and explained a new drill that would sharpen our skills. Ten players were to spread out and form a circle around a player in the middle. Taking the ball, a player from one half of the circle was to chip to the man in the middle, who had to control and then volley the ball to a nominated player on the opposite side, without letting it touch the ground. One by one, we awaited our call to the middle, and one by one, our technical deficiencies were exposed. When it was my turn, I was all over the place and was instantly dismissed by the manager. 'Look,' he groaned, 'if you can't do that, you've got no chance.' And then, putting himself on the spot, Glenn gave an exhibition of how it was done. Later, a five-a-side was organized and again, to no great surprise, Glenn was the star of the show. At the age of thirty-six, he left us in no doubt at all that he was still a class act; but while we were all genuinely impressed, no player likes to be belittled by his manager and we returned to the dressing room feeling pretty pissed off. 'That fucker is unbelievable!' one of the wags opined. 'If he was an ice cream he would lick himself!'

Hoddle didn't fancy me. He never actually called me into his office and said, 'Look son, I don't fancy you,' but I was never going to be his type of player, and I was aware as soon as he took the job that he was looking for a replacement. But, ball juggling deficiencies apart, pre-season training went better than I could ever have imagined. The overtime I put in during my holidays had made a huge difference and I regularly lead the line and was one of the fittest in the squad. A week before the season began, I scored a hat trick against Spurs in the final of the Makita Tournament and walked off the pitch at White Hart Lane with the supporters chanting my name. In almost two years at the club, that hadn't happened before: I was our best player by a streak. Now Glenn, being Glenn, probably thought: I have saved this player. He has seen the error of his ways. It's all down to me. But I knew differently.

A week later, when the serious stuff began, I was unlucky not to score with a volley that crashed off the bar, in a 2–1 defeat at home to Blackburn. I played well in our second game, a 1–1 draw at Wimbledon, but didn't get a kick when we were beaten at Ipswich; and the pressure was starting to build, by the fourth game of the season, when we played QPR at home. With just one point from three games, Hoddle needed a win to quell the rumblings of discontent; and with no goals from three games, the amnesty awarded to me at the Makita was also up for review. But cometh the hour, cometh the man reborn, and I sent them all home singing with a sweet left foot that secured our 2–0 win. In the next game, a 1–1 draw at home to Sheffield Wednesday, the renaissance continued with my best performance of the season and I woke up on Sunday morning, feeling better about myself than I had for years.

In the afternoon, Steve Wishart, my former manager at Crockenhill, invited us over for a barbecue and life was good as we sat down with a couple of drinks to shoot the breeze. I should, I suppose, have known better than to have been drawn into a match on his tennis course, but it was only a bit of fun; my opponent, Mike McLean, was a professional golfer, and how much damage could two professional athletes inflict on each other in an amiable joust? But midway through the opening set, I felt a dart of pain in my hamstring and slowly, horribly, my season began to unravel.

Three days later, I scored after fifteen minutes when we played Tottenham in our biggest game of the season. I had been carrying my leg in training in the hope that the injury would simply disappear, but before half time it was obvious I was struggling. Hoddle asked me to stay on for as long as possible as I was winning a lot of ball and still causing problems for the Spurs defence, and I managed to hold out until the final ten minutes, when I limped off the field to a great ovation. Hoddle seemed pleased with my performance after the game; with ten days to kill before the visit of Manchester United, there was every chance my injury would heal. But three days before the United game, Ireland were playing Lithuania in Dublin in a World Cup qualifier and though my first loyalty should have been to the club, I couldn't bear the thought of withdrawing from Jack's squad. Hoddle wasn't sure and insisted on a fitness test.

'Do you think you'll be OK?' he asked, when I came through unscathed.

'I'm sure I will,' I replied.

But despite continuous treatment, the injury continued to niggle me for the next three days.

On the Wednesday, I came off the bench to replace Niall

Quinn with fifteen minutes to go in the 2–0 defeat of Lithuania, then caught the first flight back to London for training on Thursday morning.

Hoddle watched me more closely than was usual.

'Are you OK?' he asked, suspiciously, when it was obvious I wasn't.

'Bloody hammy is still at me a bit,' I replied.

He wasn't pleased.

On the Saturday, we beat United 1–0, but there was no great joy in the result for me, as I was forced to limp off at half-time. Hoddle cut me in two with a glance and to be fair, there wasn't a lot I could say in defence. Travelling to Dublin had clearly been a mistake; I had taken a chance and acted unprofessionally; I had clearly stepped offside. And when you stepped offside with Glenn, there was nothing to do but accept your fate and hope that you returned in the next life as talented and as perfect as him . . .

Jack Charlton was also feeling the heat. A month after the win against Lithuania had established us as favourites to top the qualifying group, we had been taken apart by Spain in Dublin and were suddenly faced with the onerous task of having to play Northern Ireland in Belfast, needing a result. Playing at Windsor Park is never a pleasant experience at the best of times, but to have played there in November '93 was definitely the worst of times. A week before the game, seventeen people had been massacred in a bombing and a shooting; tension between the communities had rarely been as high. From the moment we stepped off the coach, we knew we were in for one long and difficult night. And so it proved . . .

To be sure of qualifying for our second successive World Cup, we needed to beat Northern Ireland, unless the game in Seville between Spain and Denmark ended in a win for either side, when a draw would suffice. Niall Quinn was selected to start up front, as he had for most of the campaign, while I watched the drama unfold from the bench, as I had for most of the campaign. Jack was popping and hissing like a pressure cooker from the moment the game kicked off. We started cautiously but began to improve in the second half, when word came through after sixty-three minutes that Spain had gone one up. The game was balanced on a knife edge. We were taking control but weren't creating chances, and with every second that passed, Jack was becoming more and more irate. For some reason, perhaps because he was closest to us on the wing, Ray Houghton was taking most of his stick. 'Look at him!' Jack exploded again. 'Look at fucking Raymond!' So I did look at him, but he seemed to be doing all right by me. A few minutes later, however, Ray made a mistake and lost possession. Jack lost it completely: 'Off!' he said, turning to me on the bench. 'Get him fucking off.' I was stunned. Was he serious? Did he really want me to run to the touchline with a board for Ray?

In the seventy-third minute, disaster struck, when Jimmy Quinn rifled a volley past Packie Bonner, to put the North 1–0 in front, against the run of play. The ground absolutely erupted. Jack spun around in disgust and immediately ordered me to get stripped. It was a cold, blustery night and experience had taught me to wrap up well on the bench. Pumping with adrenaline, I ripped off my coat, kicked off my tracksuit bottoms and unzipped my top, and discovered that all I was wearing underneath was a plain cotton T-shirt. For the first, and only, time in my career, I had left my jersey on its peg in the dressing room! Oh fuck! What am I going to do?

Jack was getting impatient and kept glancing over his shoulder. 'Come on! What's keeping you?' Until the penny finally dropped that there was something amiss. 'Where's your bloody shirt?'

'I don't know, Jack,' I spluttered. 'I think I've left it in the dressing room.'

His face turned purple. I thought he was going to have a heart attack. 'You fuccccccking idiot!'

Charlie O'Leary, our kit man, was immediately despatched

134

to the dressing room, but as he raced down the touchline, I couldn't help thinking, What if the dressing room is locked? What if the geezer who has the key is enjoying the game from the stands? Deciding I would retrieve the situation myself, I turned to Dave Kelly, who was also on the bench.

'Dave,' I said, panicking, 'just give me yours.'

'What? Do you mean swap?'

'Yeah, just give me yours.'

Jack flipped. 'Whaaat! You can't do that! You'll have us thrown out of the tournament, you fucking idiot! Charlie . . . where's Charlie?'

I have always believed that had Alan McLoughlin not equalized with a volley from the edge of the box as we were waiting for Charlie to return, there's a fair chance Jack would have chinned me, or at least changed his mind about sending me on. But Alan's goal was enough to secure the draw, and with Spain winning 1–0 in Seville, an extremely tense and difficult evening ended in celebration.

Ten days later, Niall snapped his cruciate ligament playing for Manchester City and was ruled out for the rest of the season and for the World Cup. It was a devastating blow and I genuinely felt for him, but in football, one man's poison is often another man's meat and after four years of playing second fiddle for Ireland, I was relishing the prospect of reclaiming my old position. But within days, I was sidelined with problems of my own.

If relations with Hoddle had started to cool following my hamstring injury in September, they were positively freezing by the time December came. It was a vicious circle: in order to impress Glenn, I had to get into his team. In order to get into his team, I had to play well. In order to play well, I needed to be sharp. In order to be sharp, I had to be fit. In order to be fit, I needed to train hard. In order to train hard, I needed the cartilage in my knee to function normally. And because it had long stopped functioning normally, and was acting like a pummel stone instead of a pillow, my knee was ballooning every time I played. The problems started in late September, a week after I'd shaken the hamstring injury and returned for the game against Liverpool. Desperate to stay in the team, I started 'cheating' in training and nursing it through sessions, with the result that my fitness dropped and – well, you get the picture. By December, Hoddle had given up on me, the supporters had forgotten me and my career had returned to the awful state of limbo of the season before.

A week before Christmas out at the training ground, I was jumping for a ball thrown to me by Nigel Spackman, when I felt a snap in my knee and collapsed in a crumpled heap. The pain was excruciating. My knee was locked at ninety degrees. Nigel immediately came to my aid and, in the time-honoured tradition of defying the bleeding obvious, asked if I was OK.

'My knee's fucked,' I moaned. 'Get Wardy, quick.'

Bob Ward, the team physio, arrived and I was carried back to the dressing room for a preliminary examination. The lateral meniscus – a specialized piece of cartilage, shaped like a quarter-pipe, that sits on top of the leg and cushions it against the thigh – had pulled away and wedged itself like a door stopper between the bones. 'I'm afraid you're looking at an operation,' Bob announced. And after he applied more ice, I was lifted to his car and driven to Charing Cross Hospital in West London.

After the briefest of delays, I was examined by a kindly surgeon, who explained the urgency of straightening the knee before proceeding further. To facilitate the process, a mask was placed over my mouth and nose and I was invited to take a few deep breaths of nitrous oxide, to numb the pain and relax the muscles in spasm around the knee. Nitrous oxide, or laughing gas as it is more commonly known, has also been known to act as a quasi truth serum. Within seconds of sucking in a breath, I was delirious.

Bob moved round opposite the surgeon and put his hand on my leg. He was telling me to cover my eyes. He was telling me

I wouldn't feel a thing. I brought my hands up to my face but started peeping through my fingers. Did they think I was born yesterday? They weren't fooling me.

'I see Wardy,' I laughed, giddily. 'I know exactly what you're going to do. You're going to jump on my leg, aren't you? You're going to force the fucker down.'

Bob smiled and told me to shut up.

'Look, what's the point?' I continued. 'We all know I'm a disaster for Chelsea. I have to be the worst fucking player ever to wear the Chelsea shirt.'

They started laughing.

'I mean, just look at me. Look at the fucking state of me. Do I look like a professional athlete? If the supporters could see me now, they'd be laughing their bollocks off. Wouldn't they, Bob? You've heard them. Admit it! They'd be saying: "I hope he doesn't ever play for us again." They'd be saying: "Don't you worry about getting that knee straight, doc! What you really need to do is chop the fucker off!"'

They stepped back for a moment, unable to continue. Bob had tears in his eyes. The surgeon was looking at me: 'He's a lunatic, this fellow.' When eventually they managed to straighten the knee, it was strapped into a brace and I was sent for an X-ray. Three days later, there was good news and bad news when they opened me up at a private clinic in London. The good news was that the operation was a success. The bad news was that the rehabilitation would take at least three months.

I started having a recurring dream, a dream I had never had before: a dream about love. I kept dreaming I had met a woman and fallen head-over-heels in love. Don't ask me her name or the colour of her hair or what being head-over-heels in love was like. She didn't have a name. She wasn't anyone I knew or had ever met. It was all very vague, but all very real. I'd wake up in the morning, knowing I'd spent the night with her, and look forward to dreaming of her again.

Sarah and I had been struggling for a while. The move to

Glasgow had proved as big a disaster off the field as on it and though we weren't arguing as frequently since returning to London, things hadn't really improved. Teddy had been born and there were times when we were OK but the underlying problems weren't going to change. I didn't love Sarah. I didn't enjoy being in her company. I was constantly looking for ways to escape – to training in the morning, to the card school in the afternoon, to Mac or Wish or whichever of my friends was available in the evening, and now, at night, to the woman in my dreams.

One night, during the period when I was injured, I came home late from a game of cards to discover a fire engine outside the house and Teddy's bedroom burnt out. I ran inside and found Sarah sitting with the kids, safe and well apart from a touch of smoke inhalation.

The incident shook the life out of me and after a night spent tossing and turning, I decided I would have to change. Somewhere along the road, Sarah and I had stopped loving each other, but that didn't make us different from most married couples. And it didn't mean I had to be a stranger to my sons. I would try to be a better father and spend more time at home. I would stop seeing the woman in my dreams. Love was far too complicated and obscure. You could always put a face on lust.

You always know you're in trouble at a club when the manager calls you in during the week of the transfer deadline in March and offers you a choice of where you'd like to be sent on loan. There were no shortage of suitors. The giants of the second division were all queuing up: Birmingham City, Charlton Athletic, Tranmere Rovers – the choice was mine. Or almost mine. Hoddle seemed particularly keen on Birmingham. The transfer deadline was his last chance to get me out of the door before my contract expired, and the Birmingham offer seemed to represent the best deal for the club.

'I don't want to go to Birmingham,' I told him.

'Well, you're not going to play for me,' he insisted.

'That's fine,' I said, 'but I'm not going to Birmingham.'

Now it's possible the move to Birmingham would have been the best of my career. It was certainly a better option than spending the last two months of the season with the reserves. But I didn't want to go down a division, and I didn't want to leave London, and I still believed I could get back into the Chelsea team.

On 2 April, after I had spent almost four months in the shade, my gamble paid off when I returned to the first team as a sub in the 2–0 defeat of Southampton at Stamford Bridge; with Mark Stein injured, and Robert Fleck out of form, Hoddle had been forced to offer me a recall. Two days later, I held my place for the away game at Newcastle and then the following weekend laid on both goals for Gavin Peacock in the semi-final of the FA Cup at Wembley, when we beat Luton 2–0.

I was thrilled to be back in the spotlight and my form continued to improve. At the end of the month, I scored in our 2–2 draw against Manchester City at Maine Road, and again four days later, when we beat Coventry at home. Our final league game of the season was a home game against Sheffield United. A week later, we would travel to Wembley to play Manchester United in the final of the FA Cup. On the day before the Sheffield game, I was informed by Hoddle that as Mark Stein was fit again, I would start both games on the bench. I was crushed, and argued that Mark wasn't fit, having just returned after being out for six weeks. But Hoddle was adamant he was making the right call, and when Stein scored twice on his return the following day, his decision was vindicated.

A few days later, I was sitting in the dressing room with Gavin Peacock when I made a prediction about the final.

'Hoddle is going to name himself as a sub.'

'Do you think so?' Gavin replied. 'He wasn't on the bench on Saturday. He hasn't played for a while.'

'Trust me,' I said. 'And if we're losing, he'll put himself on.'

'Naah, if we're losing, he has to put you on.'

'No, logic has nothing to do with it – you know what he's like. He's so full of himself he'll think, I can change it. I'll give you any odds you want.'

When the final came around my nap, unfortunately, proved correct. At 2–0 down, Hoddle decided to send himself on and it wasn't until after we'd gone 3–0 down, with eight minutes to go, that I was finally given the nod. At a reception the following day, he informed me that although he'd had second thoughts, following my performances at the end of the season, he had been forced to make a choice between myself and Nigel Spackman and wouldn't be offering me another contract. And that was it. A day after playing in the FA Cup final, I was suddenly out of a job. But all wasn't lost. I would put myself in the shop window at the World Cup finals and prove him wrong.

On the first Monday of June, the Irish team left Dublin in a blaze of glory for a training camp in Orlando, USA, to acclimatize for two weeks before the competition began. The weather was surprisingly poor for the first few days and our training was frequently disrupted by thunder and lightning storms. On the second or third afternoon, we were forced indoors to the gym again, when, while using a Stairmaster machine I felt my calf muscle suddenly tighten. I shrugged it off and hoped it would go away, but the following morning, when I joined the lads for the warm-up, it was as if someone had plunged a knife into my leg and within ten minutes I could hardly walk. Of the many setbacks I'd had in my career, this was undoubtedly the cruellest. I knew, pretty much immediately, that there was no way I was going to recover in time for any of our group games. And if we didn't qualify from the group, I'd be flying home from the World Cup without having kicked a ball. 'No,' I thought, 'not now. I can't afford to be injured. I'm out of a fucking job.'

The next three weeks were as depressing as I've known. When I wasn't arguing with Sarah, I was negotiating a truce in the war that had broken out between our respective families who, to be fair, had never seen eye to eye. The uncertainty over my contract was also adding to my woes. Every day I'd return from the treatment table to a fax from some third division manager, wondering if I'd give him a call. Was there no fucking end to humiliation? I used to be a million-pound player! Had it really come to this? And then, just when I was sure I had touched rock bottom, I returned one afternoon to find a message from Mike Walker, who was managing Everton at the time. I hurried back to the room and dialled the number immediately.

'Hello, Mike. It's Tony Cascarino.'

'Tony! Thanks for getting back to me, mate.'

'No problem, Mike. Thanks for the call.'

'Listen, I'm not sure what your situation is but we're really interested and would like you to come. We want to give it a real go this year. We've got Forest up the road who . . .'

As soon as he mentioned Forest, I realized that the manager I was speaking to wasn't Mike Walker from Everton but Mick Walker from Notts County. And though I tried my hardest to be polite when letting him down, I'm sure he thought I was a right prat. Blackpool called and announced they were interested. John Sheridan thought it a great move, when it was mentioned over dinner. 'Blackpool! That would be interesting, Cass. They've got a great Big Dipper, ye know!' I tried to laugh along but it was hard. I was fucked. There was no way back. And then, Denis Roach – who, ironically enough, was Glenn Hoddle's agent – called with the news that Olympique Marseilles, the 1993 European Champions, wanted to sign me.

'Sure, Denis,' I said. 'Pull the other one. No, let me guess, you are pulling the other one. What you really mean is Olympic Marsay from the Southern fucking league.'

'No, listen,' he said. 'You've heard about the sanctions they've been given as a result of the bribery scandal? Well, they've just been relegated to the second division, and because they're not allowed to buy any players, they're looking for internationals who are available on a free [transfer]. Are you interested?'

'Yeah, Denis, of course I am.'

'OK, I'll get back to you.'

A week after we had returned to England, Denis gave me instructions to phone Bernard Tapie, Marseilles's colourful and controversial president, at his home in Paris. The deal, he insisted, was basically done: 'Just phone him at this number and tell him you are "happy to play for his club".'

I dialled the number tentatively.

'H-e-l-l-o? M-o-n-s-i-e-u-r T-a-p-i-e?'

'*Oui.*'

'I-t-'-s T-o-n-y C-a-s-c-a-r-i-n-o.'

'*Ah oui*, Cascarino, yes, Marseilles, you must come.'

'Yes . . . er . . . I a-m h-a-p-p-y t-o p-l-a-y f-o-r y-o-u-r c-l-u-b.'

'OK, come tomorrow.'

'OK, er . . .'

But he had already hung up.

Chapter Thirteen
Destiny (Part 1): Fier d'être Marseillais

We are not permitted to choose the frame of our destiny. But what we put into it is ours.

— Dag Hammarskjold, *Markings*

Ever tried. Ever failed. No matter. Try again. Fail again. Fail better.

— Samuel Beckett, *Worstword Ho*

On the night before I left for Paris, I packed a medium-sized sports bag with enough clothes for a week and retreated to the bedroom with my passport and a new colour for my hair. Paul Shinners, the former team mate at Gillingham who had once doctored his age, was playing on my mind. What, I wondered, if I was to pull the same stunt at Marseilles? What if I was to arrive there tomorrow and deliberately mislead them about my age? There was no way I could tell them I was almost thirty-two! Thirty-two was the fucking knacker's yard for a striker! No one ever went to Europe at the age of thirty-two! But what if I could knock a year off my life and be 'just' thirty-one again? Marseilles would certainly be more inclined to offer me a longer contract; and I needed a longer contract – I was worried they would offer me a few months on trial or a short-term deal. So I opened my passport and with the deftest of squiggles, changed the handwritten '2' in the year of my birth (1962) to a '3', then retreated to the bathroom with the L'Oréal to dye the grey from my hair. Call it dishonest if you will, but I prefer to think of it as desperation. There had been no other offers since the end of the World Cup. It was Marseilles or nothing. I had to make this work.

On 20 May 1993, six days before they beat AC Milan 1–0 to become the first French club ever to win the European Cup, Olympique Marseille travelled north to Valenciennes for their penultimate game of the season. It was a huge game for both teams: Valenciennes were seventeenth in the division and desperately needed a win to stave off relegation, and Marseilles were pushing for their fifth consecutive title, but couldn't push too hard and risk injuries before their rendezvous with Milan. Valenciennes, a once proud steel town of high unemployment, isn't the most glamorous setting for football, but a capacity crowd packed the Nungesser stadium to watch their heroes do battle with the best team in France.

After forty-five minutes, as the teams returned to the dressing rooms at the end of a tense, scrappy first half, there wasn't much to get excited about in the stands: Allen Boksic had opened the scoring for the champions; Christophe Robert had limped off injured for Valenciennes. Marseilles lead 1–0 and it seemed just another goal, just another injury and just another Friday night in the French premier league. But then, after fifteen minutes, the teams failed to reappear. Rumours began to circulate about a problem in the Valenciennes dressing room. 'Was Boksic offside?' 'He didn't appear to be.' The referee had been summoned and was sorting it out. When the game eventually resumed and Marseilles held on to win 1–0, the focus immediately began to shift towards the big game on Wednesday. But the problem in the Valenciennes dressing room had not been resolved. In fact, at that very moment, as the legions of cheery OM supporters returned to their cars, the problem had just stepped from the showers and was about to leave the dressing room.

'They wanted to buy us off,' Jacques Glassmann, the

Valenciennes defender, announced to reporters waiting outside. 'I was offered FF200,000 if I didn't try too hard, and I'm not the only one: approaches were also made to Jorge Burruchaga and Christophe Robert.'

The 'they', it later transpired, was the OM managing director Jean-Pierres Bernes, who, acting on instructions from Bernard Tapie, had asked one of his players, Jean-Jacques Eydelie, to offer bribes to Glassmann, Burruchaga and Robert to withdraw from the Valenciennes team on the day of the game. The French Football League announced an immediate inquiry and a criminal investigation was also launched, as attention turned to the seemingly innocuous tackle that had seen Robert limp off before half-time. The Valenciennes midfielder refuted the allegations until he was arrested, four weeks later, when he decided to recant. On the night before the game, he had sent his wife to the Marseilles team hotel to collect a package, which they had subsequently buried in a garden. The package had contained FF250,000.

A year after the inquiry was launched, the league announced that Marseilles were to be stripped of their title, demoted to the second division for two seasons and prohibited from buying new players. A week later, I was contacted at the World Cup by Denis Roach. Were it not for Jacques Glassmann, that phone call would never have happened. His honesty was the reason I was heading for Marseilles, which is kind of frightening when you think about the impact it had on my life. I would never have met Virginia. We would never have had Maeva. What would I be doing now? Where would I be living? How would my career have ended?

The meeting with Tapie was scheduled for four o'clock. I was met at Heathrow airport by Peter Baines, a solicitor who worked with Denis Roach and after a brief discussion on the agenda for the day, we caught a midday flight to Paris and a cab to the seventh arrondissement. I began to feel nervous as the city's famous landmarks loomed into view. Traffic was chaotic but after a tedious crawl we eventually arrived at the gates of a palatial residence on the rue des Saintes-Peres, where our identity was checked before we were escorted inside to a waiting room. The president didn't keep us long before gracing us with his presence.

'Ah, Cascarino,' he boomed, shaking my hand with a vicelike grip.

Shorter and stockier than I expected, he dressed like a film star and gazed at you with eyes that searched for weakness like spotlights. Before sitting down to business, we were led on a guided tour of the house and as he marched from lavishly furnished room to lavishly furnished room, explaining the various periods and features, there wasn't a hint of his problems with the authorities or the fact that the house was about to be repossessed. The ultimate showman, Tapie was a master of illusion, where all that glittered was most certainly gold, but not necessarily *his* gold. The tour ended in an enormous office where we sat down to talk football as coffee was served.

He began grilling me on the goals I'd scored and seemed particularly curious as to what kind of player I was, which seemed a bit odd. Didn't he know what he was getting? Shouldn't he have been briefed on my weaknesses and strengths?

'Well,' I began slowly and deliberately, mindful of how poor his English was, 'I suppose I'm a bit . . .'

But he couldn't wait, and immediately delivered his verdict on some of the other British players who had played in France. '[Chris] Waddle: Yess! [Mark] Hateley: *Nonnnn!* [Trevor] Steven: Hmmm – *ça va!* Hoddle: YESSS! Cascarino? *Je ne sais pas encore?*'

'Well,' I said, 'I played with Glenn at Chelsea last season but to be honest I'm more like Hateley as a player . . . but with a lot more ability.'

As soon as he started laughing, I realized that I'd been had. He knew exactly what he was getting and was only taking the piss.

DESTINY (PART 1)

'Nice one,' I smiled. 'You had me going there for a moment.'

Taking advantage of the levity, I took a deep breath and passed him a sheet of paper with my contractual demands.

Two-year contract
£4000 per week
£65,000 signing-on fee
£65,000 if the club was promoted
Goal-scoring bonus
£1,500 house allowance
Moving expenses from England
The use of a car
Twelve return air fares per season

After a cursory glance, he said, 'No problem,' and dropped the sheet of paper disdainfully on to the floor. Shit! I thought, I should have asked for more. He seemed more interested in talking about football, and was on his feet now, with his hand over his crotch, hoisting up his testicles and insisting that you had to have balls to play for Marseilles.

'*Le* fight-ing Irish,' he smiled, punching me on the shoulder.

'*Je suis Irish*,' I enthused, unsure whether to emphasize the point by giving my own nuts a squeeze.

On the subject of my bonus, he promised to pay me £15,000 if I scored twenty league goals in the season and an extra £500 for every goal above that – on condition that if I didn't meet the target, I would pay the £15,000 to him.

'What you're really offering me is a bet,' I smiled.

He looked at me quizzically and muttered something in French.

'Never mind, ' I said. 'You're on.'

In Marseilles, legend has it that when the city was founded by Greeks from Phocaea in 600 BC, the first building to be raised was the Stade Velodrome. A day after meeting Tapie, as the flight from Paris looped over the city on its final approach to

147

the airport at Marignane, I scanned the myriad buildings for the mythical football stadium that was to become my new home. It was a glorious morning and from the moment I inhaled my first breath of Provence, I had a feeling we were going to get on.

Jean-Louis Levreau, the club's mild-mannered vice-president, was waiting to meet me in the arrivals hall. After posing for a couple of photographs for the local papers, we drove straight to the OM offices on avenue du Prado, where my contract was typed, scrutinized and signed. With just over a week to go before the opening game of the season, a friendly had been arranged with a local team, Endoume, for the following evening and despite vigorous protestation that I wasn't near fit enough, Levreau was adamant I make an appearance. 'Just play for twenty minutes,' he insisted. 'There'll be a lot of supporters at the game and they'll be anxious to take a look at you.' Suppressing a smile and the urge to admit that this was precisely what was bothering me, I agreed to give it a go.

I felt extremely self-conscious and vulnerable when introduced to the team. Walking into any new dressing room is never an easy experience but when you've come from a different country and don't speak a word of the language, it can be positively harrowing. During the warm-up, I miscontrolled a pass from Marcel Dib and was mortified when the ball spun off my foot and smacked me in the face. Dib started laughing. Brilliant, I thought. He must think I'm a great player. But I'd calmed down by the start of the game and gave a reasonable account of myself for the forty-five minutes I played. That a few of my team mates spoke English helped break the ice. Jean-Phillipe Durand reminded me we had met once before on opposing sides in an international in Dublin. Fabien Barthez, now of Manchester United, the youngest ever goalkeeper to win the European Cup, still had a bit of hair in those days and seemed a real live wire. Bernard Cassoni and Jean-Marc Ferrari were both very friendly and Michel de Wolf, the veteran

Belgian international, spoke excellent English and became an instant soulmate.

We trained twice a day, every day, for the next week. Sarah arrived with the kids and some extra clothes after a couple of days to check out some schools and apartments and seemed genuinely impressed. We stayed in a lovely room at my temporary home at the Concorde Palm Beach Hotel on the seafront until the day before our opening league game, when she returned to London to make arrangements for a permanent stay.

A crowd of almost 30,000 flocked to the Stade Velodrome for the visit of Le Mans. It was my first real experience of the legendary OM supporters, who were organized in different groups around the ground. There were 'the Yankees', 'the Winners,' 'the Dodgers' and 'the Fanatics', but by far the most fervent were 'the Ultras', who sat behind the south-facing goal, popping firecrackers and waving scarves that proudly proclaimed they were *'Fier d'être Marseillais'* (proud to be from Marseilles). Like most of the groups, the Ultras had a leader, who distinguished himself by *never* wearing a shirt. On freezing winter nights in places like Guingamp and Amiens, you'd find him directing the chants bare-chested, with his hand-held microphone – the ultra Ultra.

Although Marc Bourier was officially the team manager, Tapie did all the talking before the game and toured the dressing room slapping us on the back and lunging at us with grunts and hoisted testicles. 'The demotion to the second division,' he announced, 'was a crushing blow for everyone in Marseilles, but it was also an opportunity to "*montrer les couilles*" (to show we had balls).' But when the game kicked off we had the worst possible start and conceded a goal after just two minutes.

Urged forward by chants of *'Allez OM'*, for the next twenty minutes we battled for an equalizer until Marc Libbra was felled in the box and awarded a penalty. As Jean-Marc Ferreri, the team's designated penalty kicker, walked towards the ball and scooped it into his hands, I'm not sure what came over me but suddenly I was standing beside him. 'This is mine,' I said, seizing the ball from his hands. I walked forward and placed it on the spot.

'What the fuck are you doing, Cass?'

'I'm having it. This is mine.'

'Whaaat? Are you out of your fucking mind?

'No, it's the perfect opportunity to make a positive start.'

'Oh yeah? What if you miss? Thought about that? Take a look at that bloke with no shirt behind the goal. Listen to those headbangers he's winding up! They make the mob from the Shed look like sheep. You'll be crucified if you miss.'

'I don't care.'

'What do you mean, you don't care? For fuck's sake, Cass, what are you saying? Look, you're taking this "proud to be Marseillais" bollocks too far. You'll be grabbing your nuts next! Dipping croissants in your coffee! Kissing your team mates before training! Saying ooh la fucking la! You're not Marseillais! You're from St Paul's Cray remember? You're the boy who pissed in his pants, the big clumsy bastard who used to hide at Celtic and Chelsea! Have you forgotten Neville Southall and the groans of the crowd?'

'Things are going to be different here.'

'Yeah? Don't make me laugh!'

'No, I'm serious, it's shit or bust from now on. I'm going to think like a selfish bastard; I'm going to shoot every time I get a sniff at goal; I'm going to think and play uniquely for myself. I'm going to show them back in England. I'm going to shove it up their arse!'

I smashed it by the keeper into the back of the net. A week later, we travelled to Brittany for our second game of the season at St Brieuc. It was a tough, physical encounter that looked set to end in stalemate until six minutes to go, when we were awarded another penalty. Unopposed on this occasion, I smashed it by the keeper again for my second goal of the season. Our third game was away to Nancy and after fifteen minutes, I put us in front with a screaming volley that found the top corner of the net from twenty-five yards. Growing in confidence with every game, I made it four from four with the winner against Ales and five from five to earn a draw at Guingamp.

Our sixth game of the season was a friendly at home to Juventus. Tapie was like a lunatic in the dressing room. The game was being transmitted live on *Eurosport* and because Juventus were Juventus and Marseilles were an ageing, makeshift, second-division team, he was afraid we were going to get tanked. I wasn't. I wasn't afraid of anything. Sent out to face the German international Jurgen Kohler, I ran him ragged and scored both goals in our 2–0 win. Kohler shook my hand when the game was over. Four months earlier, we had played against each other in a friendly international in Hamburg. 'You're not the same guy I played last time,' he smiled, as we walked towards the tunnel. How right he was. I was fitter, faster and stronger. I was three quarters of a stone lighter. I was confident. I believed. I was *fier d'être Marseillais*.

On the Saturday after the Juventus game I scored a hat-trick in a 5–0 demolition of Dunkirk at home. Two days later we were due to travel to Athens to play Olympiakos in the first leg of the UEFA Cup and despite our handsome win in the Dunkirk game, Tapie gave strict instructions that there was to be no going out. 'I've got contacts in every nightclub in the city,' he warned. 'The moment you walk through the door, I'll hear about it.' Of that there was no doubt. Olympiakos was a huge game for Marseilles, marking as it did the return to the European stage for the first time since their historic triumph in Munich. As we ran out to warm up, I was approached by a Greek official, who asked about my plans for the following season and whether I'd be interested in coming to Athens. Tapie saw us talking and pulled me the moment I returned to the dressing room.

'What was all that about?' he asked suspiciously.

'Nothing – he's just a reporter,' I replied, not wanting him to think I was courting a move. He said nothing, but it was obvious he didn't believe me and suspected I'd been offered a bribe. For the first time since joining the club, I failed to find the target and missed a couple of decent chances, fuelling Tapie's suspicions that I'd been bought. Despite our 2–1 win, he went berserk in the dressing room.

'*Salaud! Pute! Combien tu l'as vendu?*' He was rubbing his thumb against his index finger, making the sign of money.

'Whaat!' I exploded. 'That's a bit fucking rich coming from you! Talk about the pot calling the kettle black! You're fucking mad.'

But though things got quite heated for a while, relations soon returned to normal.

Three days before the return leg in Marseilles, we were ordered to the team hotel on Sunday afternoon after training. Tapie had summoned his personal physician from Paris, and after dinner we lined up in one of the rooms and rolled up our sleeves for a 'booster' injection. I hadn't a clue what exactly the boost was and didn't feel inclined to ask. Most of the players were having them and it seemed easier to join the herd than cause a fuss. The boosters weren't the only injections at the club. Before games we were offered shots – twenty tiny pinpricks, injected into the lower back by what looked like a stapling gun. Never having seen it in any dressing room in England, I asked one of the physios what it was and if it was legal. 'Of course it's legal,' he replied. And then he smiled. 'And anyway, our doctor does all of the tests at the club.' I decided to give it a go and maybe the effect was purely psychological but it definitely made a difference: I felt sharper, more energetic, hungrier for the ball. One night, aware my lower back was starting to look like a dart board, I declined the injection before a game. Noting my reservations, Tapie brushed me aside, pulled up his shirt and blasted himself in the back.

But I don't know to this day what it was.

The return leg against Olympiakos was transmitted live on

DESTINY (PART 1)

TF1 and in front of our biggest crowd of the season, I scored twice and played exceptionally well in our 3–0 win. As a mark of appreciation, the leaders of the various supporters' clubs started wearing shirts I'd worn at other clubs – Celtic, Villa and Chelsea – to the games. The Ultras named me 'Tony Goal' and started waving Irish tricolours. People were stopping me on the streets to shake my hand and sending over drinks and picking up the tab for my meals in restaurants. The support was overwhelming. By the first week of November I had won my bet with Tapie and scored my twentieth league goal – and would score sixteen more (eleven in the league) before the end of the season. A year after my career had touched rock bottom in England, I was a star at the biggest club in France. I had finally turned it round, finally achieved my potential, finally delivered a perfect season. Well, almost perfect . . .

Chapter Fourteen
Damage

A lovely thing about Christmas is that it's compulsory, like a thunderstorm, and we all go through it together.
— Garrison Keillor, *Leaving Home*

Being divorced is like being hit by a Mack truck. If you live through it, you start looking very carefully to the right and to the left.
— Jean Kerr, *Mary, Mary*

Saturday, 18 December 1999

I spoke to Sarah today for the first time in months – which is not to suggest that we actually conversed. We haven't conversed for a while now. We spit words at each other and score points over each other and punch each other, long distance, in a verbal Morse code. This morning was pretty typical. I rang her.

'Hello.'

'It's me.'

Although I occasionally identify myself as 'Tony', nine calls out of ten I am 'me'. I'm not sure I still have the right to be me, given we've been separated for almost four years and I am also 'me' to Virginia and have never believed a man can *truly* be me to two women at the same time. And I would certainly have to stop if Sarah were to remarry. But maybe I should stop anyway. Maybe I'm just being cruel. Maybe it's just another subtle smack in our ongoing tit for tat.

'I'm coming over for the week,' I announce.

'Are you coming on your own or bringing her?' she asks.

DAMAGE

Virginia is 'her'. Virginia has always been 'her'. The tart that lured her husband. His little bitch on the side. Right up until the moment we divorced, Sarah regarded Virginia as a phase I was going through, a confusion that would clear my system. 'Stop fuckin' about,' she'd say. 'I've had enough of this game. You're coming home, aren't you? Just get yourself home.' Despite the lies and everything that had happened between us, she still wanted me home. And though much bitterness has since divided us, sometimes I think she still does.

'When can I have the boys?'

'When are you coming?'

'I'll be over on Sunday.'

'Well, you can have them on Sunday night.'

'Hold on! I said I'll be over on Sunday. I can't collect them Sunday. I need to arrange it. I'll come on Monday.'

'OK, take them on Monday, but they're with me on Christmas Day because I'm having my family around. You can have them on Boxing Day.'

'Fine! Suit your bloody self !'

So much for the season of goodwill. I don't know anyone who has had a nice divorce. You live with someone for seven years, sleeping with them, waking with them, sharing with them, and then it sours and concord turns to discord and love becomes hate and suddenly there's this distance between you as if you've never even met. I could never hate Sarah but there are times when I am hateful towards her, times when I wish we had never met.

Sunday, 19 December

One of the bonuses of the game in France is '*la trêve*' – the mid-season break. On Friday we closed the first half of our season with a 1–0 win over St Etienne at home and now have a two-week break before training resumes on 30 December. It was snowing when we left Nancy this morning and my knee was so stiff by the time we got to the shuttle in Calais that I nearly fell out of the car.

'Are you OK?' Virginia asked, alarmed.

'Yeah, it's nothing,' I moaned. 'I'm just seventy years old.'

Dover to Sevenoaks was a forty-five-minute drive. My mother was waiting by the window when we pulled up outside, which is pretty much where I expected she would be. What is it about mothers and their extraordinary devotion to their sons? I have more grey hairs than she has, but know that in her eyes I will never grow old. She is Theresa Smith these days, having taken her husband Howard's name when she married again in June 1996. Howard is a kind-hearted man with a good sense of humour that is regularly put to the test.

'Howard?'

'Yes, Tony?'

'I know Mum loves you 'n' all, but why did she change her name to Smith! Why would *anyone* change their name to Smith? She used to be one in a million but now she's one of ten million! It just doesn't make sense!'

We're staying in an annex or granny flat at the side of the house. Maeva was her usual timid self as we stepped from the car but within minutes was driving everyone mad and jumping into my mother's arms. We opened a bottle of wine over dinner and had just sat down by the fire when my attention was drawn to the Christmas tree and the card from Willo and Matt. 'Happy Christmas Theresa, Love you lots,

XX Willo and Matt.'

As I scanned a second card with hugs and kisses to Howard, I was reminded for the first time since crossing the Channel, of what it is to live in England. I don't know any country in the world where cats are as literate or treat their owners with more affection.

Mandy, my sister, phoned later and offered to collect the boys from Sarah tomorrow evening. From time to time I'll drive over to her house and pick them up myself but I've grown tired of being left waiting on the doorstep, tired of Sarah's sniping about my car and my clothes and how much money I have, and will spare myself the aggravation whenever possible.

DAMAGE

But divorce casts a very long shadow and there is often no escape.

Monday, 20 December
This morning was a typical example. After breakfast I took a trip with Virginia to my old home near Chislehurst, which I've been renting to a man from Northern Ireland, since I settled with Sarah after the divorce. I left the car outside, and was walking up the driveway towards the house when I was startled by a vision in my mind of the boys running to greet their mother on the lawn. We then went shopping in Chislehurst, where I spent the rest of the morning glancing anxiously over my shoulder, expecting Sarah to appear at every turn. My former wife and Virginia, it must be explained, have never actually met and until they do, I have resigned myself to walking the streets with this sense of dread.

The hardest moment of all, however, was the arrival of the boys this evening when I was greeted, as usual, with all the warmth of a Siberian winter. Michael shuffled his feet anxiously and managed a faint 'Hello, Dad,' while Teddy didn't even look at me and just sprinted to the presents under the Christmas tree. Maeva, who is always shy when the boys arrive, had taken refuge behind Virginia's leg and looked at me with eyes that said: '*Pourquoi, papa, ils ne courrent pas vers toi et ne te font pas de câlins comme moi?*' (Why don't they run to cuddle you like I do, Dad?') But how do you explain damage to a four-year-old girl?

Worse, far worse, than their outward lack of affection – because I am not, it has to be said, demonstratively affectionate by nature – is the barrier that goes up each time I return. It's this barrier that really gets me down. I accept it as a consequence of my actions, and understand that their first allegiance will always be to their Mum, and I know that within a day or two I will have bridged the divide, but that first contact is horrible. I can't continue living away from them like this. I do not want to end up a stranger to my sons.

FULL TIME

Tuesday, 21 December
The relationship between the boys and Maeva is another cause for concern. This morning, they were harmony personified when we drove to the Toys 'R' Us in Tonbridge. Maeva sat between them in the back and we played our usual game.

'Who do you prefer Maeva, Teddy or Michael?'

'Teddy.'

'So Teddy's your favourite, is he?'

'*Non, j'aime Michael aussi.*'

But I'm not sure it will last, because while they get on really well at the moment, it will be harder when they are teenagers and the inevitable jealousies creep in. Already there were traces of it this morning, when Teddy started comparing the price of the bike he is getting for Christmas to the Cinderella castle that Maeva wants and Michael's computer games. Before long I'll have Maeva screaming at me in one ear – '*Tu leur donnes tout, moi tu t'en moques!*' (You give *them* everything, you don't care about me!) – and the boys in the other – 'She's your *real* family! We're only second best!' But hopefully, when the football ends, I'll be able to give them time and make them understand that I cherish each with equal measure. It's not going to be easy, especially for Virginia, who will always be 'the Enemy', no matter how hard she tries. But what can you do except take it one day at a time?

Wednesday, 22 December
The phone rang early this morning. My mum came to the door and called Virginia. It was Bertrand, her brother, calling from Nancy. I turned over on the pillow and listened as she slipped downstairs. It wasn't like Bertrand to call so early and from her reaction it seemed there was obviously something wrong . . .

'*Nonnnn . . .*'

'*Mais tu plaisantes!*'

'*Ce n'est pas possible!*'

I dressed immediately and joined her in the kitchen.

'Nancy have just signed a new centre forward,' she announced.

'You're joking?'

'No, a Brazilian for twenty million francs.'

I was stunned. Twenty million francs is £2m! That's enormous money for a club like Nancy – the equivalent of Manchester United spending £40m. Laszlo Boloni, Nancy's manager, only plays with one centre forward and if they've just splashed out £2m on a Brazilian, they're not going to leave him on the bench. So where does that leave me? What are they going to do with me? After three years as the first-choice striker, am I to be condemned to the bench for the rest of the season? Fuck that! I can see things souring over the next few months. I should have got out last year; I should have quit while I was ahead. Careers in football are like divorces: there are few happy endings – they always end up bad.

Mum asked if I wanted a bacon sandwich for breakfast but for the first morning since returning, I declined and settled for a cup of tea. 'I've got to be careful now,' I smiled. 'I'd better watch my weight.' But maybe I am already history; maybe it's too late. In the afternoon, we took the kids over to the park but the weather wasn't great so we came home early and put a few Disney videos on. None was about football. All had happy endings. I was a bit subdued for the rest of the day, which is ridiculous when you think about it. I am almost thirty-eight years old; I've had a great career and played with some of the best teams in the world. But it still hurts. It still fucking hurts.

Thursday, 23 December

For almost a week now we've been planning a night on the town. Mac collected me in his brand new Jaguar at eight and we drove to my sister's house in Petts Wood to pick up the Cappuccios – Tony (my brother-in-law), Peter (my best man) and Daniel (my nephew). The plan was to drive straight to the Bull in St Paul's Cray, but as we were about to leave Petts Wood, Daniel asked Mac to stop at the cashpoint near the station. There was a small queue of about two or three people at the dispenser when Daniel left the car. I was sitting in the front with Mac and we were all looking forward to our few drinks on the town when Tony suddenly recognized a face in the crowd.

'There's Pauline,' he said.

And sure enough, when I looked across, she was standing in the queue with Daniel. Oh fuck, I thought. Come on, Daniel! Hurry up!

But Mac, who couldn't read my mind, didn't know who Pauline was and was brimming with seasonal cheer, decided he would introduce himself: 'OI! PAULINE!' he roared.

I could have hit him: 'You dopey fucking idiot, Mac! That's Sarah's mum!'

'Oh fuck! Sorry, mate!' he gushed. 'I had no idea.'

But already she was heading for the car. At first she couldn't see me in the darkness.

'Who's looking for Pauline then?'

Then she spotted me in the front: 'You!' It was the first time we'd met in the three-and-a-half years since I'd left Sarah. She looked at me with such hate that I thought she was going to punch me through the window. 'You bastard!' she spat. 'You'll get your fucking comeuppance! Your boys will know everything about you!'

Daniel grabbed his money and sprinted back to the car as if we were making a getaway, which, in a sense, we were. Mac apologized again on the way to the Bull, but though I told him it was nothing, the incident stayed with me like a cloud for the rest of the evening. That Pauline hated me was understandable, but there were two of us in the marriage and I wasn't going to accept this. I thought about phoning Sarah to complain but there didn't seem much point as I knew exactly what she'd say: 'Well, what did you expect? That she was going to give you a bunch of flowers and wish you a nice Christmas?' I drowned my sorrows with a pint. And then another. Got pissed. Had a curry.

DAMAGE

Friday, 24 December

Woke up this morning with a terrible head and decided to have a run. Bad idea. Trotted for twenty minutes but was blowing out my arse. I blame the curry. Haven't felt so bad since the double Wimpey and chips. Phoned Sarah after my shower to arrange for the boys' return and couldn't resist a little swipe.

'I bumped into your mum last night.'

'I know.'

'Isn't it funny how bad news travels so quickly.'

But not much more was said. Spent the afternoon in London, shopping for Virginia's present. Steve Wishart phoned and asked if I was interested in taking in a game on Boxing Day. Told him I would think about it.

Saturday, 25 December

I have always enjoyed Christmas. Even in the bad old days when my father was at war with himself, there would always be a Christmas week truce, when he would relax and spoil us. It was a good day. Santa called for Maeva and filled her stocking with the Barbie and castle she had asked for. I gave Virginia a necklace and was given the old-fashioned globe I had asked for, and we traded dressing gowns and slippers with Howard and Mum. The highlight of the morning was a phone call from Michael – my first ever! – who wished me a happy Christmas. I was then passed to Ted, who only wanted to talk about his bike, which I promised he could have tomorrow. At lunchtime, I nipped down to the pub with Howard – my *petit papa* – and we were joined by Mandy and Tony, her husband, for a drink. Dinner was the traditional feast: turkey, ham and the Queen's speech at three: 'A very happy Christmas to you from St George's Chapel, Windsor. Listening to the choir reminds me that this season of carols and Christmas trees is a time to . . .'

'She doesn't look very happy,' Virginia observed.

'She never looks happy,' I agreed.

But we were both shushed by Howard who, I've noticed, is

161

always very respectful of the royal family. I fell asleep after dinner and stuffed myself with turkey sandwiches in the evening. Thought of my father and his new life in America as I was slipping off to bed and regretted not phoning to wish him a happy Christmas. Would it mean as much to him as the call I got from Michael? Undoubtedly. Will call him tomorrow.

Sunday, 26 December

Decided against going to a game. I miss the English league and miss playing here, but when you've lived it on the inside, it's hard to watch it from the outside and I never feel comfortable sitting in the stands. One of the things I noticed during my last years with Ireland was how awkward retired players often looked whenever they called at the team hotel. They always stayed in reception. They never came to the rooms. I found it curious at the time but understand it now.

Howard collected the boys and we gave them their presents. Mandy and Tony arrived for dinner and we played games with the kids and had a brilliant time. I phoned Dad at his new home in Lebanon, Pennsylvania, and wished him a happy Christmas. He was going out for a meal with his wife Bernie's family and seemed in good form.

Monday, 27 December

Woke up with a temperature and diarrhoea and spent the day flicking through the reports on yesterday's games in bed. I always check the West Bromwich Albion and Manchester United results first, to see how Andy Townsend and Teddy Sheringham have done, and then look to my former clubs and to Liverpool, for whom my childhood love has endured. In Division Two, Millwall lost 1–0 at Bristol Rovers and are now just a point clear of fifth place Gillingham, who beat Colchester 2–1 at home. In the Premiership, Chelsea grabbed the headlines by being the first – but certainly not last – league side to field an entire team of non-nationals in their defeat of Southampton at The Dell. Elsewhere, Villa won 2–0 at Derby,

Liverpool drew 2–2 at Newcastle and this afternoon, in the old firm game in Scotland, Celtic were held to a 1–1 draw by their friends, the enemy. It wasn't a great day for Andy or Ted: Andy, who is starting to hate the game as much as I do, didn't play in West Brom's defeat to Manchester City and will probably call it a day at the end of the season (he resigned as a player on 8 July 2000). At Old Trafford, Teddy started the game against Bradford City but was substituted in the second half before the first of United's four winning goals which, I imagine, will probably make him feel as good as I do at the moment: bad.

Tuesday, 28 December
Crawled out of bed and had a bath and a shave but ended up crawling back for the second day in succession, which was a pity as we return to France tomorrow and it was my last day with the boys. Told Michael it was definitely my last season and that I'd soon be able to give them more time. Not sure what he made of it, not sure he understands. I can't afford to spend another year away from them. With each season that passes the barriers take longer to come down.

Wednesday, 29 December
We decided to take the boat (£59) instead of the shuttle (£163) at Calais this afternoon. The shuttle is quicker and more comfortable but I can't afford to waste £104 if I'm going to be out of a job at the end of the year. Was feeling a bit down when we arrived back in Nancy. If it wasn't for Virginia and Maeva, I would have forfeited the last six months of my contract and not come back at all.

Thursday, 30 December
Drove out to Forêt de Haye, which has been decimated by the recent storms, for training at 9.30 a.m. Felt as weak as a kitten and basically just shook hands with everyone and came home again. 'Everyone' included Ze Alcino, our new record signing from Brazil – 'Nice to meet you Ze (you bastard)' – who seemed

nice enough but looked like a fish out of water. It's always the same when you arrive at a new club and don't speak the language; you sit in the corner, shut your mouth and wait for your team mates to pass judgement on you after the first training session. The general opinion was that he looked a good player, which isn't exactly a compliment when you come from Brazil. I mean, I haven't seen a Brazilian yet who didn't look good! And they've all got names like classic fucking thoroughbreds: Pele! Ronaldo! Rivaldo! Rivellino! Jorginho! Paulo Cézar! But maybe that's just me being bitchy again . . .

Friday, 31 December
Went for a jog with Laszlo, our manager, at the training ground and was assured by him that I would remain his first-choice striker for the rest of the season, which I knew was a load of bollocks but was happy to hear. Was still feeling weak so didn't do too much, but joined the rest of the team in the dressing room when Monsieur Rousselot, the club president, arrived with a crate of champagne to toast the new year. Went shopping with Virginia in the afternoon and started drinking quite early when we got back to the apartment. Bertrand and Virginia's grandmother joined us for a dinner of escargots, poularde and Bûche-de-Noël. After celebrating the new millennium at midnight, we sat down in front of the TV and watched it happen again an hour later in England. I thought of the boys and my mother and sister and felt very homesick but kept it to myself as I didn't want to spoil things for Virginia. Tomorrow we leave for Casablanca and a week's training camp to prepare for the second half of the season, which I'm looking forward too like a hole in the head. Play it again, Sam . . .

Chapter Fifteen

Destiny (Part 2): The Territory of Lies

The curse which lies upon marriage is that too often the individuals are joined in their weakness rather than in their strength – each asking from the other instead of finding pleasure in giving.

— Simone de Beauvoir, *The Second Sex*

He entered the territory of lies without a passport for return.

— Graham Greene, *The Heart of the Matter*

My name is Tony Cascarino and I am thirty-seven years old. While I believe, deep down, that I am essentially a good man, and a decent human being, there is one chapter of my life I would bury for ever in the ground. This chapter. I am not proud of what follows and have thought long and hard about what I am about to write, and the guilt that compels me to write it. The temptation is to present myself as Tony Goal, the swashbuckling hero of Marseilles. But every morning, when I stand before the mirror, it is a different man who gazes back at me. And no matter how many times I blink or close my eyes, he never goes away.

I did not want my marriage to fail. I know too much about failure. I had watched my parents' marriage fail, had failed for long periods of my football career and was determined to stick it out rather than fail again. By the summer of '94, our marriage certainly wasn't succeeding; I was cheating on Sarah at every opportunity; we had argued bitterly at the World Cup; and the only thing uniting our families was their mutual contempt. The move to Marseilles had come at just the right time. It was a chance to clean the slate, a chance to start again.

A week after my meeting with Tapie, Sarah arrived with the boys. We stayed at the Palm Beach Hotel until the Thursday before the opening game of the season, when we decided to take a trip to Cannes to meet Andy Townsend and his wife, Jackie, who had just arrived on a week's holiday. They checked in for a night in a fancy hotel on the Boulevard de la Croissette, and after securing a babysitter to watch the boys, we booked a table for four in a brasserie beside the hotel.

It was one of those classic, balmy, summer nights when it feels good to be alive. Sarah and Jackie have always got on well and as Andy and I had not seen each other since the end of the World Cup, there was loads to gossip about. At midnight, after a really nice meal, Sarah suggested we move on to a nightclub.

'I can't stay out,' I said, 'I've got a game on Saturday.'

Sarah was disappointed. She had switched into party girl mode and when Sarah was in party girl mode she ignored all the red lights.

Andy tried to be as diplomatic as possible. 'Come on, be fair, Sarah. He can't! It's his first big game! It's important he makes a good start!'

Sarah wasn't having it. She kept pegging away . . . 'It's got nothing to do with the game.' . . . kept pushing out the envelope . . . 'It's always the bloody same.' . . . further and further . . . 'He's just a boring bastard.' . . . and she had gone over the edge.

I had been called worst things in my time, but none had ever hurt as much or popped as big a fuse in my head. I thought I was going to explode. Andy and Jackie, who had been circling the table like firefighters, were running out of water to douse the flames. We paid the bill and stepped outside and I walked on ahead with Andy towards the hotel. A cool sea breeze was blowing gently across the boulevard but it wasn't cool enough: 'I could fucking kill her,' I spat.

166

'Calm down,' he urged. 'She's just had a few drinks. Just go to bed and forget about it.'

There was no chance of that. I was walking quicker now. I couldn't wait to get back to the room, close the door and shut out the world so it was just me and her. Alone.

'You fucking bastard.'

'You fucking cow.'

'You're fucking loathsome.'

'I fucking hate you.'

I'm not sure how long we had been screaming when Michael poked his head through the door. And can't really explain why his frightened little face didn't bring us to our knees. It's just the way rage envelopes you, I suppose; short-circuiting your brain, numbing your senses, taking control so that nothing else matters. And in the early hours of that summer morning in Cannes, nothing else – not Michael's living nightmare, not my first game for Marseilles, not anything in the world – mattered but retribution from Sarah, making the bitch pay.

'I didn't have a job three weeks ago!' I fumed. 'I've been training my bollocks off, trying to secure a fucking future for us all, but all that interests you is having fucking fun!'

I reached out and shoved her on to the bed. She bounced straight back and fronted me again. She was like a pit bull; she kept biting back: 'Don't you touch me, you boring fucking bastard!'

I wanted to kill her. I wanted to drive my fist into the middle of her face. The rage began to scare me. I actually did want to kill her. I actually did want to punch her, as I had once been punched. Is this what happens when you grow up with violence? I made a conscious effort to calm down. What on earth was happening to me? I took a sheet and pillow to the bathroom and decided to make a bed.

A few hours later, we breakfasted together and it was as if nothing had ever happened. 'Morning,' she chirped. 'All right? Funny last night, wasn't it?'

It was typical Sarah. She genuinely didn't believe we had a

problem, was fully prepared to carry on as if nothing had been said. I wasn't. My sense of humour had gone. I had been doing a lot of thinking in the bath.

'I'm going to leave you, Sarah,' I said.

'Shaaat-up,' she said. 'It was nothing.'

But I was never as sure of anything in my life.

On the evening after the Le Mans game, during dinner at the Palm Beach Hotel, I found myself sitting opposite a young French couple. The girl was pretty but I didn't think much of her boyfriend. I glanced across until we had made eye contact and convinced myself she would rather be with me. I met the couple again in the bar a few hours later and started chatting. She was Virginie Masson, a 20-year-old law student from Nancy, who was living in Nice. And he was Bertrand Masson, a 23-year-old law graduate and fanatical supporter of OM. We retired to a nearby table and ordered some drinks. Bertrand wanted to talk football and the game the night before, but I was much more interested in getting to know his sister, whose name I couldn't pronounce.

'Virgin-ee?'

'Veer-gin-ee,' she corrected.

I made another stab at it but failed miserably.

'Virginia is OK,' she said.

After a couple more drinks, we decided to make a night of it and adjourned to a music bar across the road. Her English wasn't great but it was better than my French. She informed me they were returning to Nice in the morning. I took her number and told her I'd give her a call.

Two weeks later, I left Marseilles early on the morning of Sunday, 14 August, armed with directions to her apartment in Nice, which had been procured for me by my interpreter and team mate, Michel de Wolf. It was a bank holiday weekend and we spent two glorious days touring Monaco and Nice, dining in Casino Square at the Café de Paris and holding hands on the Promenade des Anglais. Sarah mocked later that it was a typical *Shirley Valentine* romance – tired English footballer has his batteries recharged by thrilling French nymph and confuses lust for love – and in the beginning it undoubtedly was. But the attraction was more than physical. There was something different about Virginia, something I had never encountered in a woman before.

She didn't want to see me again when I told her I was married and she announced that she was planning to spend the year in Tahiti with her mum. I phoned every day on my return to Marseilles and made a succession of futile attempts to get her to change her mind. After a week she informed me she had booked her ticket but agreed to see me the following Friday before jetting off.

The relationship should have ended there, I suppose, saying our farewells in tears; but the more I thought about her, the more I couldn't let go. I phoned and faxed messages every day for the next two weeks.

'No, Tony.'

'I'm sorry, Tony.'

'Forget it, Tony.'

And then I played it. My trump card. And in the first week of October, Virginia returned . . .

I was sitting on the sofa, sweating. The boys were playing in the corner, Sarah was in the bedroom, a TV was humming somewhere in the distance and five hundred yards away in another hotel, Virginia was waiting for me to fulfil my promise. My head was spinning. It had been spinning for days. I had waded into unknown territory and there was no safe way forward or back. I stood up from the chair and walked past the boys to the bedroom. Sarah was lying on the bed watching TV. I sat on the edge with my back to her. The words were glued to the roof of my mouth . . .

'Don't turn away, just say it.'

'Say it.'

'JUST FUCKING SAY IT!'

'I've got something to tell you, Sarah,' I announced. 'I've been seeing someone from Nice. We've been having an affair.'

She sat up and walked to the bathroom, visibly upset, and reminded me of a promise I had made when we were married.

'You always said you would leave before being asked if you ever had an affair.'

'Yes, I did.'

'Well?'

'No . . . I don't know . . . It's all a bit of a mess at the moment. I'm going to need a bit of time to sort it out.'

'What does that mean?'

'I don't know.'

'Are you going to keep seeing her?'

'I don't know.'

But 'don't know' wasn't good enough. The following morning she packed her bags and took a taxi with the boys to the airport. I had hoped she would make it easy for me and she had. It was over. She was gone. But the sadness of their departure rattled me and I was suddenly unsure. I sat with my head in my hands for almost an hour, then put a frantic call through to the British Airways check-in desk. Sarah was reluctant to take the call at first.

'Don't go,' I said. 'Please, I'll finish it if you come back.'

'OK,' she said.

I had won myself some time.

Virginia had no reservations about granting me a reprieve. It was enough that we were seeing each other again. Deciding she would complete her degree in Marseilles, she moved into a small apartment near the stadium and over the next six weeks, I reneged on my promise to Sarah and lived a secret double life. In the morning, I'd leave the house at eight thirty for training at ten and spend an hour with Virginia, returning when the session had ended in the afternoon for two or three hours or staying even later sometimes, depending on the pretence – a meeting, a game of golf . . . I played a lot of golf. And grew to love playing football at home when, aided by a loyal room mate armed with the number of my mobile phone, I'd sneak from the team hotel and spend the night with Virginia, sneaking back before dawn. There were a couple of minor slip-ups. One night, when I was out eating with Virginia, I mistakenly referred to her as Sarah. 'I'm Virginia, not Sarah,' she corrected, and just carried on. She was brilliant company and our relationship progressed like a train until November when she started feeling sick. Fearing the worst, we bought a pregnancy test from a local pharmacy one evening but the reading was inconclusive and we decided to try again, first thing next morning. She was stone-faced when I arrived at the apartment.

'I've already done it,' she announced. 'I'm pregnant.'

'Oh shit,' I said.

We stared at each other in silence. The stakes had suddenly been raised.

December was miserable. Although much surer now that I loved Virginia and that I wanted to make a commitment, I still couldn't bring myself to leave Sarah and the boys. Virginia announced her position. There was no question of an abortion: her child was a child of love. And no question either of a gun being placed to my head. 'Don't worry, Tony,' she assured me one afternoon, 'if you don't come with me I will have the baby on my own. I am not going to ask you to leave your wife. That's a decision you have to make for yourself.'

But I fudged for weeks and in January she announced she was returning to Tahiti. She didn't want money. She didn't want anything. Her only demand was that her child would know its father. She regretted it later, wishing she had simply disappeared . . .

Ironically, it was only after Virginia left that Sarah became suspicious. There was something wrong with her husband. He was behaving very erratically. His training schedule had changed dramatically, with later starts and earlier finishes. He had stopped going to 'meetings', had even stopped playing golf! In six years of marriage she had never seen so much of him. He was *around*! He had also developed the most irritating of habits. An addiction to buying newspapers. A craving for fresh bread. And always in the evening . . .

'I'm just popping out to get some bread, Sarah.'

'It's all right, Tony, I'll go.'

'No! You've got enough to be getting on with the dinner.'

'Well, actually I think there's some in the freezer.'

'No, it's OK, save it for later. I want fresh bread.'

But Sarah was no fool. 'Going to phone your girlfriend, then?' she smirked.

'Bollocks! Don't start that again,' I countered.

But she wasn't convinced.

The problem for me was the twelve-hour time difference with Tahiti: if I was to maintain contact with Virginia – which I was resolutely determined to do – I could phone no earlier than seven in the evening. Or send a fax. One evening, after slipping out of the door for 'an English paper to check the weekend results', I was gone for five minutes and had the phone to my ear when I noticed Sarah's Peugeot 306 cabriolet in my rearview mirror. The kids were in the back. She was signalling for me to pull over.

'Oh fuck! Sarah has followed me from the house,' I told Virginia. 'I'll try to call you tomorrow.'

I casually replaced the phone in my lap, tapped in Andy's number and pulled over to the side.

'What's wrong?' I asked.

'Give me your phone,' she demanded.

'What do you want the phone for?'

'You've been talking to your fucking girlfriend again, haven't you?'

'No,' I said, 'I've been talking to Andy.'

She grabbed the phone and pressed re-dial and Andy's number came up. Attack is the best form of defence.

'Oh for fuck's sake,' I exploded, 'you're going to make me

look a right * * *t if you start checking up on me each time I call a friend!'

She handed me back the phone.

In the last week of March, I took a flight to Dublin for a European championship game with Northern Ireland. Sarah had returned to London with the boys for a few days and made arrangements to come to Dublin with Jackie Townsend. On the morning of the game, I received a fax from Virginia with the news that she had just had a scan and was expecting a baby girl. Showing it to Andy, I rolled the sheet into a ball and placed it deliberately in the bin. After the game, Sarah and Jackie followed us back to the hotel.

The game (1–1) hadn't gone particularly well but at dinner the drink soon lightened our spirits and the night was progressing splendidly when Sarah picked a key from the table and left the room. To this day, I have no idea what happened during the fifteen minutes she was gone; I know only that she was clutching the fax when she returned. I spotted it the moment she stepped through the door, followed her slow, deliberate march across the restaurant floor and watched in trepidation as she stood at the edge of table and drained her vodka and tonic before ordering me outside: 'I want to have a word with you.'

The outlook was bleak as we marched grimly down the corridor towards the bedroom. I was a liar and a cheat. Sarah was holding the proof. There was nothing else for it but to make a full confession . . . but as we stepped through the door, I suddenly saw a way out.

'What the fuck is this?' she exploded

'It's not what you think.'

'What do you mean, it's not what I think! She's having a fucking baby!'

'No! Calm down!'

'You bastard.'

'Sarah, listen. I can explain. Do you remember the letter I showed you before Christmas? The one from the fan? The fucking nutcase with the fantasy who wanted to have sex with me.'

She was crying.

'This is the same. I'm telling you, Sarah! There is no baby! She's just another crazy fan! It's like that film *Fatal Attraction*! She is trying to destroy our lives.' Looking back, I cannot believe I said that. I was a total shit.

By morning the storm had abated. I awoke early to catch the first of two flights to Marseilles. Before leaving I went to see Andy. He took a couple of minutes to answer my knock on the door. Jackie was still sleeping.

'I think I've smoothed it over,' I whispered.

He couldn't believe it. 'You've smoothed it over! How the fuck did you manage that?'

'I told her it was a fatal attraction,' I grinned.

Yes, I grinned. Not because it was funny but because I was still on a high at having pulled it off. Take a bow Harry Houdini! Wow! What a buzz! But the effect was short-lived and by the time I'd arrived in Marseilles, I was overwhelmed with remorse. I had betrayed Sarah for Virginia. I had betrayed Virginia for Sarah. Who was next? When was it going to end?

Strangely, while my private life was in chaos, my second season was even more successful than my first, as I continued to play like a god for Marseilles . . . a contradiction I find hard to explain. Maybe it was the sheer relief of being able to leave it all behind. Maybe it was the weight I lost worrying about it. Or maybe, just maybe, I was so wrapped up in my newfound celebrity that I'd become immune to the suffering I was causing.

On the morning of Sunday, 12 August, I made a very deliberate fuss about the state of my golf clubs before placing them in my car. I'm not sure Sarah noticed. I'm not sure Sarah cared. In the five months since the discovery of the fax, we had moved to a house in Mimet and she had fallen in love with Provence. She still raged at me from time to time, and had once

174

had her wedding ring delivered to me before a game (earlier that morning, she had made a 'check' call to the training ground and had handed the ring to a groundsman – 'Give Tony this' – when informed we weren't training until the afternoon), but had almost come to accept the lies. I was just 'being famous', just doing what famous people do. She never believed I would leave; she knew I was soft.

My golf excursion, with 'some sponsors from the club', was taking me to Royal Mougins on the outskirts of Cannes. I left Marseilles at nine and took the A8 to Mougins, but ignored the exit and continued on to Nice where, two days earlier at l'hôpital de Sainte-Genevievre, Virginia had given birth alone. Her face lit up when I walked through the door. 'This is your daughter,' she beamed, and presented me with all 49 centimetres and 3 kilos of the beautiful Maeva, which is Tahitian for 'welcome'. I took her in my arms and touched her little fingers, but the moment was tarnished by the guilt I was feeling inside. What kind of father would I be for her? I hadn't seen her (we had an away game at Perpignan) for two days. I had kept her identity a secret. What kind of father denies his own child?

Virginia moved back to her apartment in Marseilles. Her mother stayed for a while but it didn't take long before the reality of single motherhood began to bite. The next few months were a lonely and depressing time. I continued to visit regularly but they were only ever visits and not nearly as exciting as before. There were no romantic dinners or nipping around for a quickie: just tears and fatigue and nappies caked in shite. Our relationship began to come under strain and had deteriorated so much by Christmas that I was actually getting on better with my wife. I wanted to be with Virginia but couldn't leave Sarah and the boys. And for months it continued until the summer of '96, when Virginia finally decided she had taken enough. She was leaving for Normandy to spend some time with her father. There would be no more lies.

My mother and Howard married on Saturday, 8 June. I

phoned Virginia from the reception but for the first time since we had met, two years earlier, she was refusing to answer my calls. The following morning, I jumped into a car and disappeared for five days until Thursday evening, when I called Sarah.

'What have you been? Why didn't you call? I've been worrying about you for days!'

'I'm in Normandy,' I said. 'I've been with Virginia and Maeva all week. I couldn't call for the obvious reason that I didn't want to upset you.'

We arranged to meet in Marseilles on Sunday. There was an initial heated argument and then things calmed for a few days, when we talked it through again and she asked me what I wanted to do. I wanted to leave. I wanted to take a chance with Virginia but I didn't have the courage to say it to her face. And I couldn't bear to leave the boys with an image of their dad walking out of the door with his bags. So I told her I was confused and needed a day to work it out, and she obliged the next morning and took the kids out of the house.

'See you later, Tony.'

'Bye, Dad.'

I waited thirty minutes before packing a sports bag with some clothes, then sat down at the kitchen table to write a note.

Sarah,
  I'm sorry. It's something I had to do. I know you will never understand.
  Tony.

If there is one day I could change, one day I could retrieve and rewrite, it is that one. Sarah deserved better. It was a spineless way to go.

Chapter Sixteen
Theresa's Secret

How simple a thing it seems to me that to know ourselves as we are, we must know our mothers' names.
  – Alice Walker, *In Search of Our Mothers' Gardens*

Irishness is not primarily a question of birth or blood or language; it is the condition of being involved in the Irish situation, and usually of being marked by it.
  – Conor Cruise O'Brien

After placing the note on the table, I closed the door, put my bag in the car and drove to Marseilles train station to meet Virginia and Maeva, who were arriving from Normandy. We spent our first few weeks together at an hotel in Marseilles, then moved to an apartment in Cassis. Sarah stayed in Marseilles for a couple of months and I kept in regular contact with the boys. I took them to a park on our first afternoon and tried to explain to Michael why I was no longer living at home, but he was only seven and just thought I had gone away for a while. They both seemed fine but I know they were affected.

Pre-season training began in early July. It was the summer of '96 and the sanctions imposed after the 'Valenciennes affair' had finally been lifted. Marseilles announced their return to Division One with a new manager, Gerard Gili, and a spate of new arrivals who included the Bulgarian star Lechkov and the German goalkeeper Andreas Kopke. Most of the old guard who had served the club well during its two-year exile were sold to make room for the talent, but they had extended my contract for another year and improved the terms. The season began promisingly with a 3–1 win at home over Lyon which was televised live but the result flattered us. We weren't that good a team and struggled over the next few games.

Ireland also had a new manager: after ten successful years at the helm, Jack Charlton had stepped down and been replaced by Mick McCarthy. My initial reaction when he got the job was, 'That's me fucked.' Mick and I had always got on well (apart, it must be said, from one blow-out at Italia '90, when he'd taken umbrage at my demeanour after I'd been dropped against Egypt and ordered me to 'get yer fucking chin up') but I wasn't getting any younger and I didn't think Mick had a place for me in his plans. In August, however, I was called into the squad for the opening game of our World Cup (France '98) qualifying campaign in Liechtenstein. On the eve of the game, we submitted our passports for inspection but were informed by officials of a change in the FIFA rules, stipulating that all players had to be citizens of the country for which they had declared. I had always travelled under a British passport (the one with the doctored '3') but resolved to apply for an Irish one after being giving an exemption for the game. Liechtenstein aren't exactly Brazil but 5–0 was still a positive start, given the cloud hanging over us from a calamitous 0–0 at the same venue a year earlier. I watched from the bench until the last five minutes, when I was sent on for Andy, who had picked up a knock.

The next morning, I stopped off in London and spent a day with Mum before travelling on to Marseilles. When I mentioned the problems in Liechtenstein and informed her I was applying for an Irish passport, she seemed slightly uneasy.

'What do you need a passport for?'

'Because they've changed the rules and if I want to play for Ireland again, I'm going to need an Irish passport.'

'Oh, right.' Mum paused.

'There's something I've been meaning to tell you,' she said. And it was at this moment, in the kitchen of her home in

Sevenoaks, that I discovered I wasn't qualified to play for Ireland.

Deep down, from the time she was a child, my mother always suspected there was something wrong. Little things, like her place of birth, bothered her: why had she been born 'away' in Watford, when her three older sisters had been born at 'home' in St Paul's Cray? And then there was the rumour about her mum. None of the neighbours had ever noticed that Mrs O'Malley was pregnant. She had gone away for a couple of weeks and arrived home one afternoon with a baby girl – Theresa – who she was calling her own! The whisper had fuelled my mother's doubt. Was Michael O'Malley from Westport *really* her father? Was Agnes O'Malley from Watford her natural mum? The years passed and her parents grew older and she continued to shy away from the answers until the night Michael died, ten years after Agnes, in 1982. My mother was with him at his deathbed, having cared for him diligently in the last years of his life. Maureen, her sister, had accompanied her to the hospital.

'Just tell me one thing: am I really his daughter?' my mother asked her sister.

'No, you're not,' her sister replied.

My mother was devastated.

Three summers passed and nothing more was said until I arrived home from training at Gillingham one afternoon, buzzing with the news that I'd been contacted by the Football Association of Ireland.

My mother was pleased but a touch reserved. 'What links do you need to have?' she enquired.

'It's all set up,' I enthused. 'Grandad qualifies me to play for Ireland! I just have to apply for an Irish passport, so I'm going to need copies of all the birth certificates and stuff.'

A few days later, I took a train to Victoria station and submitted an envelope with the relevant documents to the Irish embassy. A week passed. Nothing happened. I made some phone calls. The process was 'ongoing'. Still nothing happened. I travelled to Dublin for the Jimmy Holmes testimonial; made my international début against Switzerland in Berne; played the Soviet Union at the Lenin stadium in Moscow; was trounced by Denmark at Lansdowne Road – but still there was no word from the embassy. And then, finally, the envelope arrived and they were all there, all my mother's documents, everything . . . except the passport and a letter saying it had been declined. It seemed a bit odd but I didn't follow it up. I didn't need to. I had won three international caps. And for the next eleven years, I continued playing for Ireland with my British passport until the Liechtenstein game in 1996, when FIFA changed the rules.

'Why didn't you tell me?' I asked.

'I couldn't,' she replied. 'I didn't know the rules and wasn't sure if you'd qualify. Michael wasn't your grandfather, but you were his only boy. You know how proud he would have been if he'd seen you play for Ireland.'

The next few weeks were difficult. I returned to Marseilles and considered announcing my retirement. In the past, whenever the cynics had smirked, 'How can a Cascarino play for Ireland?' five proud words had always sufficed: 'My mother is Theresa O'Malley.' But that had suddenly changed. My mum wasn't an O'Malley as I'd always believed. I didn't qualify for Ireland. I was a fraud. A fake Irishman. I phoned Andy for advice.

He was amazed: 'For fuck's sake don't mention a word to anyone,' he said. 'No one is going to accuse you of not giving your best. Just apply for the passport and sit tight.'

September drifted by and our second group game with Macedonia was approaching. I would do the honourable thing: inform the FAI and quietly retire. And then I thought: Why should I? What had changed? Michael was, and would always be, my grandfather as far as I was concerned. I had always given 100 per cent to the team. How could a player who had been to

180

two World Cups and earned sixty-four caps suddenly not be qualified? I asked my mother to post all the birth certificates, as requested, to the FAI and decided to brave it out. On the first Saturday of October, I joined the team in Dublin. We trained in the afternoon and again the following morning, and on Sunday evening, I was taken to a local police station to have my application for a passport signed and witnessed. I had expected an immediate inquisition – was sure the discrepancies in the birth certificates would be spotted and my application refused – but there were no further questions. And on the day before the game, the elusive document was handed to me at the team hotel.

Passport: IRELAND
Surname: Cascarino
Forename(s): Anthony Guy
Date of birth: 01/Sep 1962
Date of issue: 08/Oct 1996
Nationality: Irish
Place of birth: GBR

I was an official Irishman.

Two days later, on a windy night at Lansdowne Road, I made my sixty-fifth appearance for Ireland. As luck would have it, Niall Quinn was injured and Mick sent me on from the start, and I walked out burning with desire to honour my grandfather's memory and my newly acquired citizenship. One up at half-time, I scored my thirteenth international goal less than a minute into the second half, when I got behind the defender following a flick from Keith O'Neill and beat the keeper with a sweet left foot. But my second goal of the evening, twenty minutes from the end, gave me much more satisfaction. Jeff Kenna sent a great ball over from the right and I met it with one of my trademark headers and buried it in the net. When it was over, and we had won 3–0, I was absolutely buzzing when I was applauded off the pitch and awarded 'Man of the Match'. And the headline in the *Irish Independent* next morning, captured my sentiments perfectly. 'CASCARINO ON THE DOUBLE: Recalled ace repays faith as Macedonians crumble.'

If they only knew.

I didn't play much over the next two months. My knee had been giving me trouble since the start of the season and I wasn't hitting it off with my manager, Monsieur Gili, who didn't believe I could score in the top division. In December, I was offered a move to bottom-of-the-table Nancy, which didn't really appeal at first. On the plus side, it was a chance to extend my career for an extra season and to prove Gili wrong. And on the minus, it meant a cut in salary and moving from the temperate glory of Provence to one of the coldest cities in France. Virginia swayed it in the end. Marseilles had brought us together but it had also almost driven us apart. Nancy would be good for us.

Chapter Seventeen
Full Time

The extent of one man's guilt may be defined by how much of it is experienced by the party he injured.
                    – Ryszard Kapuscinski, *A Warsaw Diary*

You can be young without money but you can't be old without it.
                    – Tennessee Williams, *Cat on a Hot Tin Roof*

Tuesday, 9 May 2000

Nancy has been good for us. Better than we ever imagined. When we first arrived, a lot of supporters were sceptical, believing that I had just signed for the money and would just sit out my time, but I scored a hat-trick – my first in Division One – in my second game and played so well for the remainder of the season that Gili was hammered in Marseilles for letting me go. For the last two seasons, I have continued to give my best for the club and tonight, in recognition, I was awarded the Medaille D'Or – the highest honour the city can bestow – at a champagne reception in the Marie. It was lovely. Virginia's family are from Nancy and it was a great honour to join a list of previous recipients that included the city's favourite son, Michel Platini. All the team were present: I was showered with tributes from every angle and was so overcome that I almost lost it in my acceptance speech, when I announced that 'the perfect ending for me would be to score the goals on Saturday that kept Nancy in Division One'. I'm not sure that Jacques Rousselot, the club president was listening. At the end of the evening, he asked me to rip up my contract and stay for another season. I thanked him for the offer but refused.

Wednesday, 10 May

The contract to which he was referring is the one I signed last month, committing me next season to Red Star, a third division team in Paris. OK. I know. How can a 37-year-old pro who has made eighty-eight appearances for his country, played in two World Cups and spent the last sixteen chapters moaning about the state of his knee, how much he misses his boys and how badly he wants to quit even consider another year? Never mind another year at a club where the average gate is 600 people! Fear is how. Desperation is how. Money is how. What other job was going to pay me as well? What else was I qualified to do?

My first contact with Red Star was a phone call on 31 March. Three days later, I sat down with the club president Jean-Claude Bras and was offered £50,000 up front and a monthly salary of £7,500, which was half what I'm earning at Nancy, but over three times more than the average wage in the division. Thanking Monsieur Bras for his interest, I told him I needed a week to think it over, but within an hour I had made up my mind. I wasn't signing for Red Star: I had too much self-respect to drop two divisions. I would break out the hair dye and request a meeting with Jacques Rousselot and cut a deal to spend a final season at Nancy.

Monsieur Rousselot nodded studiously when informed of the Red Star offer and listened intently to my assurances that I hadn't yet signed. In an impassioned five-minute speech, I thanked him again for all the success I'd had at Nancy, expecting that at any moment he would thrust a new contract at me and implore me not to do anything rash. But he just sat in his chair, nodding until I had finished, when he stood up and offered his hand. Stunned, I walked back to the car and phoned Virginia.

'Well,' she asked excitedly. 'What did he say?'

'You're not going to believe it,' I replied.
'What? Tell me?'
'His exact words were, "*Bonne chance*."'

Thursday, 11 May
The following weekend, I scored twice against Strasbourg – my
first goals in over a month. Monsieur Bras was impressed and
suggested another meeting. We talked plans and tactics first,
and the role they had envisaged for me: I would play with two
quick lads alongside, who would get the ball in the box. Then
the discussion switched to money.

'The offer you've made isn't enough for me to play at that
level. I want a £60,000 sign-on fee; £20,000 bonus if we're
promoted; a year's rent up front and £12,000 a month.'

'Will you sign for that?' he asked.

'Yes,' I replied, surprised.

He paused for about a minute and consulted an assistant.
'OK,' he said.

I've scored again since and Nancy have come back with an
offer but I've done the deal with Red Star and won't go back on
my word. Laurent Moracini thinks I'm mad. 'You should have
held out for a deal. You're still good enough to play in the first
division.' Maybe he's right. Maybe I am. But it's by no means
certain that Nancy are going to stay up.

Friday, 12 May
Laszlo has abandoned the Novotel Houdemont. After a string
of bad results that have sent us tumbling into the relegation
zone, he decided a fortnight ago, before our last game with
Nantes, that there was better luck to be had elsewhere, and so
this evening, while our opponents, Auxerre, were arriving in
Nancy, we drove an hour down the motorway to stay at an
hotel in Metz. It's my last time to room with Cedric Lecluse,
whom I've always regarded fondly, even though tonight, as
usual, he was never off the phone to his wife. She's worried
about the game. A lot of the wives are. Cedric is staring at a 20

per cent pay cut if we are relegated tomorrow and a £25,000 bonus if we win and stay up. Under the terms of my contract, I'll make double that again, but the Red Star deal has insured me against failure, so the stakes are definitely higher for Cedric and the boys. And the outlook isn't great. I've had a bad feeling about the game all week: we should be good enough to beat Auxerre but I'm not sure we're going to get the break we need elsewhere. Marseilles, Nantes, Rennes and Troyes are the four other teams on the trapdoor. Marseilles will stay up with a point at Sedan, who have nothing to play for. Nantes will stay up if they beat the already relegated Le Havre. Rennes will stay up if they win at home to Metz. And Troyes will stay up if they earn a point at home to Paris St-Germain, who also need just a point to qualify for the Champions League. Our destiny is out of our hands.

Saturday, 13 May
Nancy 2, Auxerre 0

We got to the stadium an hour and a quarter before kick-off. The crowd was already starting to build when I ran out to warm up. A group of schoolchildren were skirting the pitch with a massive banner that said, 'Merci Tony.' The ovation from the fans quickened my heart and sent goose pimples sprouting all over my skin. I returned to the dressing room thinking: 'I have got to repay their faith in me.' Laszlo issued his final instructions and had a word for each of us as we exited the door. Normally he just lets me get on with it but tonight he made a point of stopping me: *'Encore une fois, Tony,'* he said.

Ze Alcino followed me on to the pitch. In the five months since his arrival at the club, he has struggled to make an impact and scored just three goals. We've played up front a couple of times together but never really gelled. Tonight Lazlo was deploying him as a winger, which I felt happier about. He is not making the most of his talent and needs to work harder on his condition. Sometimes, I've looked at him slouching around the field and been reminded of myself in the bad old days.

The first half was difficult. We worked hard and had most of the possession but created very few chances. A lot of the spectators had come to the game with radios. When we returned to the dressing room at half-time, it wasn't looking great . . .

Le Havre – Nantes 0–1
Sedan – Marseilles 2–2
Rennes – Metz 0–0
Troyes – PSG 2–2

The half-time from Rennes was the only glimmer of hope, but as things stood, we were relegated, unless we managed to win. Laszlo encouraged us to keep working hard and to be patient. Laurent Moracini was more direct: 'Come on, Tony,' he said, slapping me on the shoulder. 'We need a goal.' Three minutes into the second half, Ze sent a great ball across from the right and I headed home to open the score. The stadium erupted. It was five minutes past nine and Rennes and Metz were still tied. If the scores remained the same until the end of the game, we would stay in Division One. Two minutes later, we could tell from the reaction in the crowd that Rennes had gone ahead. Winning wasn't enough. We needed one of the other four other teams to slip up. With twelve minutes to go, I scored my fifteenth goal of the season with a header from a free. No one left the field when it was over. We stood huddled in little groups, waiting for the results from the other games. They all went against us.

We began walking disconsolately towards the dressing room. An official requested that I give a final salute to the fans. I set off around the stadium but didn't know whether to laugh or cry. I have scored four goals in my last five games, finished the season with the sixth best scoring record in Division One, been honoured this week as never before – but the perfect ending for me has been tarnished by the devastating blow of relegation of the team.

Laszlo shook my hand when I returned to the dressing room. There's a fair chance I'm not going to meet him again. There's a fair chance I'm not going to see Cedric or Laurent or 'X' or any of them again. Football is like that. Here today, gone tomorrow – we make many acquaintances but few friends.

Sunday, 14 May
Was up early this morning to pack for our return to London. There was a lot of packing: gear for my testimonial next week in Dublin; clothes for our wedding two weeks later; and more clothes for the holiday we've planned to Tahiti. We'll be away almost six weeks in all. Decided to damn the expense and take the shuttle at Calais and got back to Sevenoaks in the early afternoon. Mandy brought the boys around in the evening.

Michael handed me a note from Sarah: 'You need to speak to Michael. He doesn't want to go to your wedding and doesn't want to see you the week before the wedding. Don't force him to go and don't be angry with him. My mum can look after him on the day and for the week before if that suits.'

Upset, I followed Michael to the garden to have a word.

'Look, Michael,' I said, perhaps a touch too sternly, 'if you don't want to come, you don't have to come but why don't you want to see me the week before?'

'Because you might force me to come,' he replied.

'Of course I wouldn't! Don't be ridiculous! What would you do if Mummy was getting married?'

'I wouldn't go.'

'OK Michael, but one day Mummy will get married. We've all got to move on.'

But he was adamant he wasn't coming. And I didn't want to push. Teddy, meanwhile, was chasing Maeva around the garden.

'Come 'ere, Teddy,' I said. 'Are you coming to the wedding?'

'Oh yeah,' he replied.

'And why do you want to come?'

'Because there's cake and Teddy Sheringham will be there . . . I love cake.'

He makes me laugh.

Monday, 15 May

The note concerning Michael wasn't the only one I've had from Sarah recently. A month ago, I phoned her one night to speak about the boys and an argument developed when she accused me, not for the first time, of being a bad father. And I reminded her, not for the first time, about the constraints of my job. Within minutes it had turned quite heated and I started to lose control. I told her I was getting married, playing it like a trump card: 'Take that.' I should have been more sensitive. I could tell straight away she was hurt.

'Why are you getting married?' she asked.

'Because I want to get married,' I replied.

'Do you *really* want to get married?'

'Yes! I want to get married.'

'So you love her, then.'

'Of course I bloody love her.'

'OK, bye.' And she hung up.

A week later, she sent me a card, wishing me the best of luck for the future and acknowledging that it was time to move on and forget the past. And I was just about to phone and thank her for the gesture when I reached the bottom line: 'You finally have what you've always wanted – a housewife!' She was almost there, she was almost magnanimous . . . but her wound is deep. And I have no right to complain.

In March '97, I called to collect the boys one afternoon, while on a flying visit to London. Eight months had passed since I'd walked out of their lives and they had returned with their mother to our old home in Chislehurst. They were playing in the garden when I arrived and followed me into the kitchen when Sarah invited me inside.

Relations between us had been thawing for a while. I pulled

out a chair and Sarah filled the kettle for tea and as I sat, staring at the remnants of my family, I was suddenly overwhelmed by an uncontrollable grief. Sarah gave me a hug and asked what was wrong. I tried to explain the guilt and the emotional fog that was choking me, but am not sure I made sense. I stayed for a couple of hours. Sarah was kind and sympathetic and I continued to call whenever I was home; sometimes staying for an hour, sometimes staying longer. The fog slowly cleared and after a few months I decided to end my visits. There would be no more personal contact. I was sending the wrong message. I phoned to tell her that in future I'd be sending someone else to collect the boys but the damage had already been done . . .

'Stop playing the game now, it's getting on my nerves.'

'What game?'

'You're having a laugh. Stop fucking about.'

'How do you mean?'

'You're coming home, aren't you?'

'No! I'm not!'

'I've had enough of this game. Just get yourself home.'

I find it hard to live with the fact that I lied so much to Sarah. I'm not sure I could forgive her if she had done the same to me. She has decided to leave the country for the week of my wedding. Nothing would please me more than to hear she has found someone and is happy; someone who is better for her than me.

Tuesday, 16 May

I flew to Dublin this morning to begin preparations for the testimonial I'm sharing with Steve Staunton on Sunday. It was good to be back . . .

'Howysa goin, Toeknee.'

'It's yourself, Toeknee.'

'All set for Sunday, Toeknee.'

Ten years have passed since the heady days of Italia '90 but we are still treated like stars. On my most recent visit, I was invited on to a radio show and the producer was amazed at the

FULL TIME

amount of calls from older women. The sons all want to meet Roy Keane but the mammys love the oldies – Cascarino, Staunton and Quinn. I wouldn't have it any other way.

Jean-Pierre Hoch, a journalist from our local paper, *L'Est Republicain*, phoned as I was driving into the city with the news that Laszlo has been sacked. I expressed surprise but it wasn't unexpected. The last few months have been torture for him and his family. It's a horrible job.

Wednesday, 17 May
Testimonials are not all they're cracked up to be. With just four days to go before our game with Liverpool, we are currently in debt to the tune of over £300,000. I wouldn't have believed it unless I had seen the figures.

IRFU fee (use of Lansdowne Road) – £50,000
Ticketmaster fee – £24,500
FAI Player Fund – £16,333
Insurance – £50,000
Event management – £35,000
Team expenses – £22,500
Stewarding – £16,000
Marketing – £15,000
Security – £25,000
Accountancy fees – £5,000
Catering – £5,000
Security advertising – £5,000
Cleaning of Lansdowne Road – £8,000
Miscellaneous (FAI) – £3,300
Players' gifts – £3,000
Medical expenses – £1,400
Miscellaneous – £20,000

We need a big crowd on Sunday or else we'll be picking up the tab. There is no way I would have accepted the game without Steve on board and the next few days are going to be worrying.

FULL TIME

A few years ago, Packie Bonner brought Celtic over and was sweating right up until kick-off. Liverpool haven't done us any favours with the way they've finished the season but they're still Liverpool and they're bringing most of their stars . . .

Thursday, 18 May

Steve, or Stan, as we have always called him, has worked tirelessly over the past few months to make the game a success. I first met him in 1988, when he was called up by Jack for a friendly against Tunisia. He was nineteen years old at the time and a few months away from an FA Cup winners' medal at Liverpool, where he was understudy to Ronnie Whelan, Ray Houghton and John Aldridge – not, mind you, that Stan saw it like that.

Fiercely independent, Stan looked up to nobody and I vividly recall his dismissal of Ronnie – who was the Liverpool captain at the time – one night when he was ordered to 'fetch' a round of drinks for the boys: 'Fuck off.' If there is one thing I have always appreciated about him, and indeed about Niall and Kevin Moran and all the Irish-born lads, it's that they never regarded us as inferior Irishmen. We were always a team.

Friday, 19 May

I called at the team hotel this morning and joined up with the squad. A lot has changed in the six months since November. I'd watched Stephen McPhail on TV but never met him before and Dominic Foley from Watford was a complete stranger to me. One or two of my former team mates were still going strong. Niall shook my hand and immediately went on the attack.

'How many have you sold? I bet you've been counting them? You must have sold at least 20,000 tickets! *And* the [weather] forecast for Sunday is good. You lucky bastard.'

Robbie Keane, who had adopted me during my last months with the squad as his source of bedtime stories, wanted to know if I'd any new ones to tell. And finally, there was Jason

McAteer, who was his usual, boyish, lovable self. He calls me a 'ledge', as in 'legend', which always makes me laugh because he's a much bigger name than I am. I told him I had written about the episode in Limerick when I walked into the room he was sharing with Phil Babb and thrown a skidmarked training slip to his fans.

'I hope you said it was Babbsy's,' he laughed.

Saturday, 20 May
This evening, most of the people who matter to me in life arrived on the same flight from London for the game: Virginia, Michael, Teddy, Maeva, Mum, Howard, Mandy, Tony Cappuccio, Peter Cappuccio, Daniel Cappuccio, Dominique Cappuccio, Steve Wishart, Lynn Wishart, Brad Wishart, Bertrand Masson, Chris 'Mac' McCarthy, Doug Forrest, John Hibbitt, John Maloney . . . and last, but by no means least, my dad and his wife, Bernie.

We last met three months ago at my mum's in Sevenoaks, when he returned from the United States for Mandy's fortieth birthday and I spent the evening, watching from a distance and marvelling at how much he had changed. When he wasn't pouring drinks, serving food and washing dishes, he was organizing an outing with Howard (they get on like a house on fire) and bantering with Mum. It was strange but in twenty-five years, I had never seen them so happy in each other's company and I asked Mum at the end of the evening if she was considering hitching up with him again. 'Well,' she laughed, 'he's better than the one I've got.'

My father stayed for seven years in London after my mother left in 1985. He spent almost a year with me, then moved to a house of his own in Dartford. He abandoned the building trade for a jewellery stall in the market, which seemed to do quite well. My father was never afraid of work and always had money in his pocket, but there wasn't a lot else happening in his life so he decided to open a new chapter in Lebanon, Pennsylvania, where he had some cousins who were involved in a confectionery business. He met Bernie shortly after arriving and has been *'bien dans sa peau'* (content with himself), as we say in France, ever since. He comes home at least once a year and Howard has planned to go back with him after the wedding next month. Mum still feels resentment towards him sometimes when she sees him playing with Maeva and the boys: 'Why couldn't he have been like that with his own kids?' But I just marvel at his ability to change and learn from his mistakes. Finally, after all these years and all we've been through, I look to him now and find inspiration.

Sunday, 21 May

As I am no longer officially an international footballer, I've been staying with my family at the Burlington Hotel in the city, rather than with the rest of the team at the airport. Liverpool are also here and Stan arranged for me to share their pre-match meal as I hadn't had the opportunity to thank them. I had a good chat with Gerard Houllier and had played against Titi Camara and Rigobert Song in France but wasn't that familiar with many of the others. The lobby was packed with fans when we left at 1:30 for the short drive to the ground. Mick and the lads hadn't yet arrived. It was the first time I had ever been in the dressing room on my own. I walked to my usual place in the corner and sat down, reminded of the great moments . . . well, actually no, that's bullshit. To be totally honest there was just one thought in my head: would the fans turn out? Would the ground be full? Were we going to earn a few quid? I'm not sure if it's just me or whether it was the same for Packie Bonner and Kevin Moran and some of the others who've had testimonials in recent years but I actually found it hard to concentrate on the game. It's like sitting in the back of a taxi in London or Paris or Rome; you're surrounded by marvellous sights and architectural wonders but you hardly notice because you can't take your eyes off the meter!

The team arrived ten minutes later and we changed and ran out. It was a beautiful afternoon and the fans were streaming into the ground. As I returned to the dressing room, I passed a small, gaunt boy with a tube coming out of his nose, sitting in a chair by the side of the pitch. He was seven years old, a Liverpool fan and attending at the behest of the Make a Wish foundation. I thought: 'You've walked straight past that boy and not even stopped to have a word! Too busy counting your fucking money!' I backtracked and shook his hand but felt disgusted with myself. Life can be so unfair.

I watched the first half of the game from the sideline. Mick McCarthy had asked me on Friday how long I wanted to play, and I'd asked him to send me on for the last thirty minutes. I had, after all, a reputation to live up to in Ireland: I was, and always would be, 'the man who comes off the bench'. I steamed on to a great reception and scored twice. The goals meant a lot to me as it was pretty competitive and my family and friends just loved it. When it was over, and I had showered and changed, I was making my way back to the hotel in heavy traffic when I decided to abandon the car and walk.

But I hadn't walked five yards when I was approached for my first autograph and then this man ran across with an outstretched mobile phone, beseeching me to 'have a word with the wife'. And for a moment, just a moment, it was almost like the days when we were kings. Almost.

Epilogue
Encore une fois

Every morning I walk to the toilet, look in the mirror and tell myself I'm the baddest muthafucker alive. But I always flush before I leave, so I can't be that bad.

– George Clinton

I open my eyes to the sound of footsteps in the courtyard, crunching on the pebbles beneath the bedroom window and then fading into the distance. A gentle summer's breeze parts the curtain. It is Sunday, 4 June and the morning is calm and sunny and warm. Virginia is sleeping beside me on the pillow. Yesterday we were wed.

We've come through a lot these last few years and there were times when I wasn't sure we'd make it. How could it be otherwise when the foundation of our relationship was two years of lies? Yesterday we started with a new sheet of paper and this morning, despite a somewhat muzzy head, I feel *bien dans ma peau* and know we will succeed.

The wedding was nothing lavish, just a small gathering of family and friends. That Michael didn't come was the only blemish, but there was cake and Teddy Sheringham and we partied all night. Andy Townsend also made the trip but presented me with a three grand appearance fee. To no great surprise he spent most of the evening, huddled in a corner swapping gossip with Teddy until I insisted they put the ball away. We love the game but don't ask us to admit it.

Tomorrow, we leave on honeymoon to Tahiti until 29 June when I've to report to my new club Red Star for work. I've put on at least a stone in the last few weeks and will have to get my running shoes on or work hard sexually: I know which one I'll prefer. It's important I return to France in the right frame of mind and conduct myself as professionally at Red Star as I did at Nancy and Marseilles. I don't want it to end badly. I don't want to let anyone down. But most of all, I don't want to let myself down because, at the end of the day, that's really all that counts. We win, we lose, the manager bangs the table. But we answer to ourselves.

Postscript

On 19 August 2000, Tony Cascarino terminated his contract with Red Star and announced his retirement after being substituted in only his second game of the season: 'The team were an absolute disaster.' A week later, Nancy made him an offer to return. He refused.

Acknowledgements

Writing books is the closest men ever come to childbearing.
                                                          – Norman Mailer

I was working on the proof of one of my poems all the morning, and took out the comma. In the afternoon I put it back again.
                                                          – Oscar Wilde

In October of 1994, three months after I had watched him limp dejectedly from the World Cup, I spent two days in the south of France with Tony Cascarino, piecing together the story of his remarkable transformation at Marseilles. He was living in a hotel near the Vieux Port with Sarah, Michael and Teddy and about to move to a house near Aix-en-Provence. I was extremely taken with Sarah but Tony seemed distant. He had just scored twice in the UEFA Cup against Olympiakos and seemed lost in his own private dream while his wife and kids orbited like satellites.

On my second evening in the city, we went for a stroll down along the sea front to the Vieux Port, where he asked me to wait a moment as he slipped into the hotel opposite the harbour. After fifteen minutes he emerged and waved to a woman on the sixth floor. He never explained who Virginia was and I never asked but the picture is clearer now. A week earlier, she had returned from Tahiti. A few days after that, Sarah had packed her bags and walked out with the boys. An hour later, Tony had phoned the airport and begged her to return. And a few days after that, the sportswriter from Dublin had arrived to paint his shiny, happy, portrait of a perfectly balanced life.

A year ago, on the eve of Tony's last game for Ireland, we sat down in the lobby of a Turkish hotel to discuss another portrait. But when Tony broached the subject of a book, I wasn't overly keen. I liked Tony and had always enjoyed his company but books about footballers are ten a penny and I wasn't prepared to commit to the usual garbage and lies. Oddly enough, neither was he. We started the interviews and the chapters began to take shape and I soon decided that ghosting Tony wasn't going to be enough. I wanted to *be* Tony. I wanted to think his every thought. But there was more to him than I'd ever imagined. His truth was as strange as fiction and more difficult to write . . . well, that's my excuse anyway.

We've spent a lot of time of time in each other's heads these last nine months and though we're sick of the sound of each other at the moment . . .

'Do you have any idea what a moody, grumpy bastard you can be at times?'

'No Tony, I have no idea.'

. . . I know we will continue to be friends. He stands taller in my esteem than ever, but I'm probably biased. Thank you Tony for sharing your little voice . . .

I owe a huge debt of gratitude to Adhamhnan O'Sullivan, the sports editor of *The Sunday Independent*, who sent me to Marseilles to interview Tony on my first assignment for the paper and who has been a joy to work with (except on Saturdays) ever since. Were it not for his patience and under-standing, the book would never have been completed. I am also deeply indebted to Aengus Fanning, the editor of *The Sunday Independent* and to Independent Newspapers for their fantastic support.

Treasa Coady at TownHouse has never published a book with so much sweat and so many swear words and provided encouragement at a time when it was needed most. Thanks

ACKNOWLEDGEMENTS

also to Ian Chapman at Simon & Schuster and to the brilliant Martin Fletcher, whom I was extremely fortunate to inherit as an editor.

Nick Pitt understands writing and writers better than anyone I know and helped unravel some early knots. His recently published *The Paddy and The Prince* was an inspiration. I also looked to Michael and Brid O'Braonain and my brother Kevin for guidance. Paul Hyland rescued a chapter that went awol from my laptop. Dr Gary O'Toole helped me get to grips with the inner workings of the knee and the truth about laughing gas. Sean Ryan checked most of the dates, facts and figures (so blame him) and my thanks also to Howard Smith for the maintenance of Tony's scrap books.

I've been absent from a lot of friends this year. Apologies to Pat Nolan and family, David and Mary Walsh, Gary and Sorcha O'Toole, Tom Humphries, Dermot Gilleece, Gwen Knapp, Tommy and Doreen Reilly ('Doreen, it's finished!'), June Williamson, Dave Hannigan, Paul Hyland, Paul Howard, Dion Fanning, Evelyn Bracken, Billy Stickland, Craig Brazil, Matt Quinn. And *mes amis français* Gerard and Muriel Torres, Andre Chappuis and Jean-Michel Rouet. A special thanks also to Alan and Valerie Stephenson and to Ray and Annette Leonard for filling in for me on holiday.

Most of the book was written in my parents' house. Thanks to Da (Christy) and Ma (Angela) and to the rest of Kimmages: Raphael, Deborah, Kevin, Aileen, Christy Jnr and the kiddies: Tara, Sean, Ciaran, Dermot and Oisin. And finally, thanks to my wife Ann ('I've taken Tony's advice and promise never to be unfaithful') and to our children Evelyn, Eoin and Luke . . . See you soon.

Paul Kimmage, September, 2000

Paul Kimmage was born in Dublin in 1962. He was a professional cyclist for four years, riding in the Tour de France three times. He became a journalist whilst chronicling his life as a professional cyclist and now works as a sports writer on the *Irish Sunday Independent*. His first book, *Rough Ride*, won the William Hill Sports Book of the Year Award. He lives near Dublin.